DREAMING OF UNICORNS

From incubation to exit – the trials and tribulations
of a tech entrepreneur's journey

CHARLIE BARLOW

QUARTET BOOKS

Published by Quartet Books
Quartet Books
Water's Edge
Charlotte Quay
Dublin 4
Ireland D04 N2W8

© Charlie Barlow 2025

Charlie Barlow has asserted his right to be identified as the author of this Work in accordance with the Copyright, Designs and Patents Act 1988

Author photo: Claire Barlow www.clairebarlowphotography.com
Chart on page 172: Shiju Kattarkandy

www.quartetbooks.co.uk

ISBN: 978-1-0684077-1-0

Typesetting by Tetragon, London
Printed and bound in Sweden by ScandBook AB
Distributed by Turnaround UK.

All rights reserved. No part of this publication may be copied, reproduced or transmitted in any form or by any means without permission of the publishers.

To Claire, for your unwavering patience and kindness and for allowing me to pursue my dreams.

CONTENTS

Foreword   xi

1. Go Big or Go Home   1
2. Solve a Real Problem   17
3. Build for Success   33
4. Culture Is Everything   55
5. Will It Make the Boat Go Faster?   77
6. Ready for Take-Off   105
7. Get Your Space Boots On, This One's Going to the Moon   127
8. Blackbox Mansion   151
9. The Honeymoon Period Is Over   171
10. Things Start to Unravel   195
11. The Wheels Come Off   219
12. Limping Over the Line   239
13. Conclusion   253

Further Reading   267
Acknowledgements   269

'UNICORN': First popularised by venture capitalist Aileen Lee, founder of Cowboy Ventures, a 'unicorn' is a term used in the venture capital industry to describe a privately held startup company with a value of over $1billion.

'Risk more than others think is safe.
Dream more than others think is practical'

**HOWARD SCHULTZ,
CEO OF STARBUCKS**

FOREWORD

I immediately recognised a kindred spirit the day I met Charlie. Healthcare innovation is never easy. It affects people's lives, challenges tradition, forces regulatory change and requires a relentless belief in a vision that, at times, only the founder can truly see. I was truly inspired by Charlie's vision and his willingness to learn. He is a tenacious entrepreneur whose courage and conviction has ultimately reshaped the way healthcare is delivered in one of the world's most complex regions, the Middle East, where he is the pioneer of telehealth.

I know this journey well. A few years earlier, in the United States, I had the privilege of leading Doctor on Demand, one of America's earliest and most successful ventures in virtual healthcare. We, too, faced sceptics, outdated regulation and the inertia of a centuries-old healthcare system reluctant to evolve. What struck me about Charlie's story was how much harder it was in the Middle East, where no regulatory framework existed for telehealth and where access to primary healthcare for millions – particularly blue-collar workers – was often inadequate, expensive or inaccessible.

Charlie didn't just launch a business. He pioneered a movement. He did so with humility, courage and an unyielding focus on solving a real, urgent problem. In *Dreaming of Unicorns*, he captures not just the strategy and operational challenges of building a telehealth company in the Middle East but the human stories and moral imperative behind it. That's what makes this book so powerful.

Telehealth today is no longer a futuristic concept – it's an essential part of global healthcare infrastructure. The COVID-19 pandemic accelerated what many of us had long believed: that virtual care could increase access, reduce costs and improve health outcomes on a massive scale. In 2024, the global telehealth market is valued at over $140 billion and is projected to surpass $380 billion by 2030. In regions where healthcare infrastructure is strained or where distances and economic disparities limit access, telehealth has proven to be not just a convenience but a lifeline.

Yet long before telehealth became a global buzzword, Charlie was battling the system. He was drafting regulatory frameworks with regional governments, engaging health authorities and advocating for vulnerable populations whose healthcare needs were routinely overlooked. He built a technology platform that not only served the affluent but deliberately extended care to blue-collar workers – people who make up the backbone of Gulf economies but whose access to healthcare had long been inequitable.

What impressed me most was that Charlie did all this with integrity and humility. He listened before speaking. He adapted when challenged. And when doors were slammed shut, he found a way to open them again. In many ways, *Dreaming of Unicorns* is as much a guide to principled, purposeful entrepreneurship as it is a business memoir.

As an entrepreneur and physician myself, I firmly believe healthcare needs more founders like Charlie – individuals who combine business acumen with empathy, and who are driven not just by

FOREWORD

opportunity but by the belief that health is a fundamental human right. Too often, innovation in this sector focuses on profit margins and exit strategies. Charlie's story reminds us that the most transformative businesses are born out of a desire to solve meaningful problems for real people.

This book is also a testament to the power of resilience. Healthcare startups are notoriously difficult. They're heavily regulated, capital intensive and emotionally taxing. Success in this field requires not just a good idea, but an unwavering belief in the mission, a thick skin and the ability to lead teams through both triumphs and setbacks. Charlie's honesty about the challenges – the regulatory dead ends, the sleepless nights, the fundraising difficulties – makes this book not only inspiring but refreshingly authentic.

Since the first day we connected, Charlie and I have shared countless conversations about the future of healthcare. What began as mutual professional respect has evolved into a lifelong friendship built on shared values and a vision for a healthcare system that works for everyone. I am proud to call him a friend, and even prouder to see his story brought to life so vividly in this book.

For aspiring entrepreneurs, *Dreaming of Unicorns* is a must-read. It offers a front-row seat to the highs and lows of building a healthcare business from scratch in one of the world's most challenging regulatory environments. For those already operating in the telehealth space, it serves as both a roadmap and a reminder of why this work matters so deeply.

Charlie's journey is proof that one determined individual can spark lasting change, and that with enough tenacity, humility and moral clarity it's possible to reshape industries and improve lives.

The future of healthcare will be written by people like Charlie, and I, for one, am grateful he took the risk.

Read this book. It may just change the way you think about healthcare, entrepreneurship and the true meaning of impact.

DR PAT BASU, FORMER CHIEF MEDICAL OFFICER OF DOCTOR ON DEMAND AND WHITE HOUSE ADVISOR UNDER PRESIDENT BARACK OBAMA, 2025

1

GO BIG OR GO HOME

'The way to get started is to quit talking and begin doing'

**WALT DISNEY, FOUNDER OF
THE DISNEY CORPORATION**

'Charlie Barlow. How the fuck did you get into my office?!'

And so it began – my journey as a first-time entrepreneur, having lied my way into the office of Dr Pat Basu, co-founder of one of the world's most successful digital healthcare companies. With a growing sense of both trepidation and excitement, I'd found myself in the heart of Doctor on Demand's San Francisco headquarters, hoping to kickstart my copycat MedTech business for the underserved, low-income populations of emerging markets.

But how on earth did this meeting even happen in the first place?

I knew next to nothing about technology or healthcare when I began the journey of incubating Health at Hand, the digital healthcare business I would go on to sell some five years later.

*

I was on a night flight from Singapore to Dubai in early 2016 when the idea first came to me. A brainwave. Or so I thought. Smartphones were becoming more and more prevalent, and WIFI was beginning to reach even rural communities in much of the developing world. I've always had an active mind for scheming and brainstorming and, having spent the last ten years living in Asia and the Middle East, I was acutely aware that in many developing markets, the quality of healthcare available to the general population often fell short of the standards found in more developed regions. What if there was a mobile-enabled technology solution that allowed patients and doctors to communicate through video – and from their smartphones? I could alleviate one of the world's great injustices, ensuring that access to quality primary healthcare was not only available to the privileged few, but to everyone. Build an app; download it on to an iPad; throw that iPad into a shanty town or refugee camp, and I'd be a world-beater.

It all sounded so easy.

In case you are asking, I had spent much of that last week in Singapore attempting to sell wireless charging units to bars and hotels for Chargifi, a UK company in which I had recently acquired a minority stake. Staying in my regular Airbnb property in Singapore, cruising the city in Ubers and enjoying my newly acquired skill of paying for drinks via my smartphone, I was embracing some of what technology had to offer in 2016. I'd previously lived in Hong Kong and was constantly amazed at how Asia seemed to be so progressive compared to Europe when it came to the adoption of innovation. Changi Airport in Singapore, for example, seemed light years ahead of European airports in terms of the customer experience and has long held its reputation as the world's most advanced when it came to cutting-edge technology. From the ChangiQ app, a queue-management platform enabling passengers to schedule when they conduct their check-in and security screening, to PlayPass, allowing them to plan various activities such as shopping and dining as they navigated their way through the airport, Changi offered a consumer experience that was, and still is, the envy of other airports. In keeping with Singapore's reputation as one of the cleanest countries in the world, the airport even developed the Where2Clean app for its staff, intelligently mapping out where teams should prioritise their time based on passenger movements to maintain a spotless building.

Intoxicated, no doubt, by the altitude on my flight home and the unlimited supply of alcohol afforded even to those in economy seats on my Emirates flight, I believed for a minute that I could become the next technology billionaire.

As my plane came in to land at Dubai International Airport, I closed my laptop, having written a thirty-plus-page PowerPoint document over the previous seven hours. At the time, WIFI was not readily available, even on Emirates' A380 planes, and as I proceeded to disembark the aeroplane, I logged on to the 'DXB free Wi-Fi' and Googled 'mobile-enabled video healthcare'.

To my shock and horror, I discovered that 'telehealth' (I was quickly informed that this was the colloquial word for the delivery of healthcare through technology) was already prevalent in many Western markets and was making waves in the United States, in particular in the delivery of non-emergency, primary healthcare. However, with a sense of undampened optimism, I navigated passport control, made my way to the nearest Costa Coffee in the airport terminal and ordered myself a large americano as I continued my research.

It turned out that telehealth was not only a 'thing', but it was changing lives and having a hugely positive impact on the delivery and accessibility of primary healthcare across the globe – everywhere except, it seemed, in the market I knew best, the Middle East. By now I was five years into my Dubai adventure, having moved there from Hong Kong with my then fiancée, now wife, Claire at the tail end of the 2008 global financial crisis. I had become disillusioned with the banking sector, to which I had devoted the first sixteen years of my career, and was ready to take a risk or two. I had a huge interest in technology businesses and had admired from afar how the likes of Uber and Lyft had disrupted the ride-sharing space and Airbnb the homestay market. What if I researched the hell out of telehealth in more mature markets, put together a team to build a proprietary, yet localised, telehealth solution for the Middle Eastern markets and set about democratising primary healthcare in the region?

I had seen how our Sri Lankan housemaid, Rasica, was treated when it came to healthcare and education. Whereas my employer paid for comprehensive international healthcare for myself and my family, Rasica was not only unable to afford private healthcare, but when we purchased it for her, being from a developing country she was treated like a second-class citizen and often asked to wait longer than others when picking up a prescription or having a regular check-up with her doctor. The Middle East, and Dubai in particular, was a land of contrasts, with an almost tangible delineation between the haves and the have-nots.

I had witnessed first-hand many of the brilliant innovations to hit the Middle East before other regions. Some of its engineering was the envy of the world, exemplified by the recently constructed Burj Khalifa, the tallest structure in the world at 163 floors, and an amazing driverless metro train-line that stood on stilts and ran the length of Dubai's main artery, the Sheikh Zayed Road. But this was juxtaposed with an archaic social welfare system, a cripplingly expensive education sector and a healthcare infrastructure that was improving at a much slower pace than the growth in population required. Perhaps this was an opportunity to build a business where profit and purpose could thrive together. Was there a chance to solve this regional challenge, the severely inadequate access afforded to most of the Middle East's population when it came to primary healthcare?

It wasn't the first idea I had had on a whim. Claire will tell you that every few months I'd have (and still do) a fabulously crazy business idea. Rather than doing the sensible thing and quickly realising that it's just that – a fabulously crazy business idea – I tend to buy a string of domain names (often in the middle of the night), before diving into developing a brand bible and business plan. I love visualising the look and feel of a new business and tailoring the branding to the desired consumer. I love coming up with names for these new businesses and designing logos. I don't know quite how extensive my GoDaddy account is, but I must have bought literally hundreds of domain names over the years. From developing concepts for low- and no-alcohol gin brands (the 'NKD Drinks Company') to social networks ('The Wire') and training schools for housemaids and cleaners ('The Academy'), I had always been keen to scratch my itch and set up my own business.

Somehow, Doctor4U (the name I originally gave it from my Emirates airline seat) seemed different. The idea fulfilled the two requirements I sought:

1) It was mobile enabled, with the ability to 'touch' millions of lives (we all have smartphones these days, don't we?). I had always dreamt of building a low-margin, high-volume business, with a desire to impact large swathes of the population.
2) It was exposed to a hugely defensive and seemingly recession-proof sector: healthcare. There was no way that healthcare spending in the Middle East would do anything other than increase over the next ten years, particularly if population-growth forecasts were anything to go by. I predicted huge increases in government healthcare spending and a significant influx of international private healthcare companies into the region.

Perhaps this was one of my hare-brained ideas that was actually worth pursuing further – and so that's exactly what I did.

Despite spending the first sixteen years of my career in banking, working for the likes of Morgan Stanley and HSBC in London, Hong Kong and Dubai, I had always held an ambition to start my own business. It was on my bucket list. But there is never a good time to embark on such a dream – or so everyone kept telling me. I, however, had different ideas: undeterred by the fact I had three children, aged six, four and two, and was living in Dubai, where school fees were becoming prohibitively expensive and taxation was slowly being introduced, I decided with my never-say-die attitude that now was as good a time as ever.

I gave Claire a quick call. I desperately wanted to go to San Francisco, the global 'home' of telehealth, if I was to properly research this idea. And three days later, there we were, disembarking at San Francisco International Airport, armed with just a smattering of meetings in my diary and a large dollop of enthusiasm.

I'd spent nearly every minute of the preceding seventy-two hours researching the great and good of the Silicon Valley telehealth scene. 'Go big or go home' is a well-known phrase as an exhortation to go all-out and be bold, but no less effective for its popularity. The idiom may well have originated as a sales slogan for a Southern California motorbike parts company, as some believe, but I prefer the theory that it comes from mogul skiing in the 1980s, where skiers goaded each other into tackling increasingly challenging runs with the phrases 'go hard or go home' and 'go big or go home'. Whatever the source, the sentiment remains the same, and my philosophy has always been that if you are not the smartest in the room, you can always be the hardest worker.

I started by researching telehealth in Western markets and realised that the US was far more advanced in this space than elsewhere. Digital healthcare companies seemed commonplace there, and solving real problems in the sector through technology was a common trend, from drug delivery and remote monitoring, all the way through to cancer diagnosis and treatment. This proven problem-solving capacity could be adapted to the Middle East, where the economic challenges of a population boom meant there was a demand for finding more efficient and lower-cost ways of delivering services, and the governments of the region were embracing public-private partnerships to drive real change, at speed.

In my opinion, the Middle East did not appear as promising to outsiders as it did to its residents. I observed that many who lived in the region, especially in Dubai, perceived it as the centre of the world, largely due to the immense wealth pouring into real estate and infrastructure projects. This perspective may have contributed to a sense of complacency, leading the region to overlook potential sources of inspiration outside their borders and hindering local innovation.

Perhaps as a consequence, the Middle East was not always a terribly exciting option when considering where to expand for those with operations in more developed markets. The population of the region was not supportive of the ambition of some of these established and growing US telehealth companies, for whom Asia, Europe, or even Africa presented a more exciting opportunity if they were to scale outside of their home market. My intuition, however, told me that this in itself presented an opportunity. If Western telehealth companies were not focused on launching in the Middle East, they may well be interested in acquiring a Middle Eastern telehealth company in a few years' time, particularly one that had managed to scale across the full region. Doctor4U would do the hard graft by launching in a number of relatively low-population countries across the Middle East, and a large US incumbent would then buy the business once I had scaled it to a meaningful size.

The access to people you can gain in today's joined-up, social-media-powered society is remarkable, if you try a little. Whereas previously it would have been nigh on impossible for me to directly message the CEOs of America's largest and most successful telehealth companies, the impossible has been made possible through the advent of LinkedIn and other platforms.

People use different social media platforms for different things, and I am no exception. I unashamedly use LinkedIn to collect contacts like they are going out of fashion. I have no concern for whether I have a personal relationship with my connections or not, and I am of the opinion that if you have an 'open' profile on

LinkedIn, you are effectively 'open' for business. Over the years, this strategy has stood me in good stead. In this instance I not only used social media to tap up the great and the good of the telehealth world, but when they didn't reply themselves, I tapped up their colleagues, friends and, as you will soon find out, in some instances I even tapped up their partners to access them.

San Francisco was an eye-opening place to visit. Anyone with aspirations in the technology world will tell you that they crave a trip to 'San Fran', and the city did not disappoint. Taking in the mesmerizingly crooked Lombard Street, the dramatic and beautiful Golden Gate Bridge, the view across the water to Alcatraz Island and riding enchanting cable cars, I conducted my own whistle-stop tour of the city on the first full day of my visit. I stayed at the trendy Hotel Zetta, which billed itself as a 'creative hotspot and cultural launchpad', and soaked up much of what San Fran had to offer. I could completely understand the hype.

It was fascinating to witness the transformative effect technology was having on daily life as I walked the streets. Passing row after row of electric car chargers, paying for coffees via my newly acquired Apple watch (what's a trip to the US if you don't visit one of the museum-like Apple stores and have a splurge?) and zooming across the city on electric scooters, it was hard to deny that the US really was streets ahead in the technology game. And then, of course, there was healthcare. Migrating something as sacrosanct as healthcare to video had so far been perceived as a step too far in Europe, and certainly in the Middle East. But in San Francisco, as I spoke to baristas, cable-car ticket collectors and hotel receptionists, there was a seemingly deeper trust for telehealth than anywhere else in the world. It worked. If it was safe and convenient, and if it meant you could see a doctor from the comfort of your own home via your smartphone, freeing up your time and reducing the cost, what was there not to like?

Of the numerous people I spoke to, about 90 per cent had heard of telehealth and close to 75 per cent had both tried and liked the experience. From a young mother on the tram, who had connected with a doctor in the middle of the night when her son had an ear infection, to a diabetic retired bank teller, who ordered his monthly insulin online, telehealth was making an impact. It would get my mind thinking about the 'consumer behaviour change' and how I would go about influencing the way people not only accessed healthcare in the Middle East, but how they might begin to trust these new methods. These thoughts would mould some of my questions during my upcoming meetings.

Day 2 was 'Game Day', and I had to get my game face on. Having left a career in banking a few years before, I was now comfortable with not wearing a suit and tie for business meetings, but what was the correct business attire in San Francisco? Too 'Mark Zuckerberg' (all T-shirts and hoodies) and I could be seen as being overly confident and disrespectful, and too corporate (jacket and tie) and I could be seen as being too formal and like a fish out of water. I went for my tried and tested, go-to business attire of an open-neck shirt and jacket – very British former public-school boy trying to be casual and possibly a total giveaway that I was indeed a fish out of water.

I had prepared well. And having used LinkedIn to arrange meetings with a C-suite of telehealth leaders in the city, I was wise to have done so. Being a novice in the sector, I had researched extensively the individuals I was meeting, not stopping at their corporate profiles but accessing multiple articles they had either authored or been quoted in. I read numerous blogs and listened to podcasts they had contributed to and, most importantly, I downloaded their apps and conducted my own video consultations on their platforms. It's so important to research well in advance of a meeting, and it's amazing how useful my minor hay fever allergy became as I connected to tens of doctors across tens of apps to learn more about their onboarding of patients, their user experience and their clinical pathways.

One thing I learnt from my 'cold' approach to accessing these telehealth leaders is that if you are respectful, humble, knowledgeable and keen to make a difference, doors will open.

I also quickly learnt that doctors are on the whole good people. Those I encountered did not seem primarily motivated by financial gain in their healthcare work; rather, they practised medicine for one simple reason: to have a positive impact on people's lives.

Another tactic I employed to acquire meetings with these strangers was throwing in a huge dollop of flattery, perhaps complimenting them on a recent article they had authored or an award they had won, information that I had gleaned from scouring the internet and the likes of LinkedIn. I was also seen as unthreatening, particularly given my geographical focus was thousands of miles away from the west coast of the US, and I made sure to mention that I was open and willing to learn. The seas parted with this approach and my list of meetings was as impressive as I could have hoped for.

No meeting is a bad meeting, if you at least ask the right questions. For the first five minutes of each interaction, I consciously tried to show off my knowledge of their business. I had researched hard and well; I knew their products inside and out and could ask relevant and impactful questions. The respect I gained from having researched their businesses was immediately evident and in turn meant that these healthcare leaders would open up to me with more and more advice and pointers. I was amazed by the support and warmth I received.

I continued to tread the boards in San Francisco into Day 3, meeting some truly inspirational digital healthcare leaders and soaking up all this newfound knowledge in preparation for my return to the Middle East. At the end of each meeting, I respectfully asked for introductions to other sector leaders (remember, no meeting is a bad meeting), and each time, the request was granted. Slowly, I was building up an enviable black book of major players in digital healthcare.

At the end of the day, Claire and I on a whim decided to hire a car to take us to Napa Valley, ninety minutes away, for the night. Booking a brilliant hotel through the ingenious app HotelTonight (subsequently acquired by Airbnb for >$400m), which amalgamated unused hotel inventory for the current night and sold it at a significant discount to normal rack rates, we found ourselves staying metres from Michelin-starred restaurant The French Laundry and the nearby Domaine Chandon winery in Yountville.

We returned to San Francisco the following afternoon, and by now I felt I completely 'got' the attraction of the city: a significantly more laid-back vibe than the likes of New York and Los Angeles, a thriving café-culture, some brilliant bars, a coastline to die for and arguably the world's most happening technology scene.

On researching telehealth as I had, there was one stand-out telehealth entrepreneur who I just had to meet. Dr Pat Basu was President and Chief Medical Officer of Doctor on Demand, a six-year-old telehealth company that on the surface looked and felt like everything I wanted to build. Doctor on Demand was a Silicon

Valley darling. Their seed funding was so well received by the market that they could count the likes of Venrock Capital and Richard Branson as early investors.

As I dug deeper, Pat's story became increasingly compelling. The son of Indian immigrants, his parents arrived in the US in the late 1960s with just $8 in their pockets and an unwavering belief in the American Dream. What makes Pat's journey even more remarkable is the modesty of his roots – his father came from India's industrial working class, and his mother was one of thirteen siblings. Pat began his academic path studying engineering at the University of Illinois, later pursuing medical training at Stanford and completing an MBA at the University of Chicago. More than this, however, Pat's LinkedIn profile had a photo of him inside the Oval Office standing next to President Obama. Digging a little deeper, it turned out that Pat had previously been a 'White House Fellow and Advisor', named by President Obama as one of only thirteen White House Fellows during the 2010–11 season and serving as a full-time assistant to a high-level government official with top-secret security clearance. If this guy was receptive to meeting me, I could learn an immeasurable amount about the global telehealth landscape and, at the very least, name-drop him into conversations when I returned to the Middle East.

By now I had developed an unhealthy 'man-crush' on Dr Pat, ever since first stumbling across his profile. Pat, however, was the only person who had so far declined my approach, and this made me want a meeting even more. I was intrigued by his story, his background, his journey. I loved everything I had read about him and the way he spoke about changing people's lives. Undeterred by the fact he didn't reply to my numerous LinkedIn messages, I found him on Facebook and messaged him that way. My wife quite rightly reminded me that I had only been researching the sector for three days and that he may well be on holiday, but I was like a dog with a bone. 'I can't build this business on my own,' I told her. I needed the insight and mentorship of those who had done it successfully before me.

And then the proper stalking started. The kind you can possibly get locked up for. I found and befriended Pat's girlfriend Kelly on social media and began messaging her via my Instagram and Facebook accounts.

As we crossed the Golden Gate Bridge back into town on the way from Napa, I thought I'd have one last go at securing a meeting with Dr Pat.

My conversation went something like this:

DOCTOR ON DEMAND RECEPTIONIST: 'Good afternoon, it's Megan here at Doctor on Demand. How can I help you?'

ME: 'H, h, h, hello, my name is Charlie Barlow. I have a meeting with Dr Pat scheduled for four-thirty today.' (I was trying my best to disguise my nerves at this complete fabrication.) 'I am running a bit late and wondered if you would kindly let Dr Pat know I won't be there until nearer quarter to five?'

MEGAN: 'I am really sorry, Mr Barlow, we don't seem to have your meeting in the diary. But . . . Dr Pat will still be available to meet you, if only for thirty minutes, before he has another meeting. We look forward to seeing you then.'

I had done it! A first minor victory in my entrepreneurial journey: a meeting with Dr Pat of Doctor on Demand fame. I quickly updated the sat-nav and headed for Spear Street.

KEY TAKEAWAYS

- **Be brave.** What's the worst that could happen? If you don't ask, you don't get. Don't leave room for any regrets further down the line – it's often what you haven't done, rather than what you have, that will hinder what you can achieve. Taking my example, organising a trip to San Francisco and arranging a handful of meetings with digital healthcare leaders was absolutely out of my comfort zone and my domain of expertise, but the fact I did it was transformational to my journey and business.
- **Use social media to directly access influential contacts.** We are so lucky to live in the twenty-first century – the world is a much smaller place today than it once was. Use technology to access people who previously would have seemed unreachable. Aim high. Try to speak to the very best and most experienced people out there in your sector. They can only say no.
- **Flattery can open many doors.** When seeking a meeting with someone who appears to be your superior, it's essential to research their background beforehand. Tailor your approach to include genuine compliments about their achievements or expertise. People are naturally more receptive and approachable when they feel appreciated.
- **Be ambitious.** If you're not positive about your business idea at the outset, you never will be. Shoot for the stars. Focus on building something brilliant rather than something mediocre. All successful businesses start with just an idea – and those who have been successful before you are no better, no brighter and no more driven than you are. So, you'll kick yourself if you don't at least shoot for the stars on Day One.

2

SOLVE A REAL PROBLEM

'Fall in love with the problem, not the solution'

URI LEVINE, WAZE CO-FOUNDER

Caught between anticipation and apprehension, I made my way out of the lift at the Doctor on Demand offices and proceeded to the reception desk to be greeted by a woman I assumed to be Megan. The reception area led into an open-plan office with desks and chairs for about fifty staff. It was a rather unremarkable place – surprising given Doctor on Demand's recent financial success and the positive press coverage they were receiving. I was expecting at least one ping-pong table or a swing chair, but perhaps these guys were serious players, more focused on 'doing' than on following the archetypal route of other early-stage technology businesses and spending money on unnecessary toys.

I was ushered into a glass goldfish-bowl boardroom and found it remarkable to see none of the white coats one would normally associate with a doctors' surgery. The scene was one of a casually dressed, diverse looking team of high-energy staff, busying themselves at the end of a working day.

In my working life I had always been in client-facing roles. It was a conscious decision I made after leaving university, and I remember my career advisor recommending that I either try my hand at being a real estate broker or a private banker given the level of face-to-face interaction involved in each role. I had read Business Management at the University of London, and private banking seemed a much more appropriate career path for me than real estate.

By the time I reached San Francisco I had conducted hundreds of face-to-face meetings over the preceding ten-plus years, particularly in my capacity as a private banker to several high-net-worth individuals, including members of the British Royal Family and tennis and Formula One stars. In theory, I was comfortable in this kind of environment and was as well prepared as I could have been, having played with the Doctor on Demand app constantly for the last few days. Nonetheless, I was still nervous as I impatiently waited for Dr Pat to enter the room.

Five minutes turned into fifteen, and my sweaty palms became progressively worse. And then, out of the corner of my eye, I spotted him. Dr Pat. Walking towards me. The guy whose video interviews I had listened to at length. Whose appearances on Dr Phil's television show I had pored over. And whose girlfriend I had messaged repeatedly, with no reply. And then it came – the first thing he ever said to me:

'Charlie Barlow. How the fuck did you get into my office?!'

Wow! The good news was that he knew my name – not surprising given the volume of messages I had sent him in the last few days! The bad news, though, was that he looked pretty pissed!

'Dr Basu,' I said. 'Thank you so much for sparing the time to meet me. I only want to take up thirty minutes of your day, but I've been desperate to talk to you and learn from your experience of building Doctor on Demand.'

Flattery gets you everywhere, and Pat's tone immediately softened, particularly as I reeled off all I knew and liked about Doctor on Demand and their app and how I unashamedly wanted to replicate much of his business, albeit for the vastly different and underserved audience of the Middle East, targeting a client base that would pose no threat to him.

By now, Pat was interested. He respected the fact that I had done my homework, and even the tenacity I had shown to blag my way into his office. From what he said to me, Pat was also a man who clearly cared about improving healthcare outcomes and access. My words had struck a chord with him. He was not only receptive to my ambition, but he was utterly charming and helpful, offering some high-level advice about how I might go about building such a solution.

It was evident from my meeting that Pat was not a tech guy. His knowledge of Doctor on Demand's technology stack was limited, a relief given I too was no tech expert. But he came across as a visionary. A strategic thinker. Someone who cared deeply about improving outcomes, no doubt influenced by his amazing backstory as an Indian immigrant in the US. I was intoxicated by the empathetic way he spoke, how he listened to everything I said – actually listened – and then offered some wonderful advice on how I might start building my own business and transforming access to primary healthcare for Middle Eastern populations.

Pat impressed upon me that I should take time to:

1) Understand the problem and build a solution that addresses it.
2) Garner support from the government and regulator by selling the benefits to them.
3) Determine who pays for healthcare in the Middle East and tweak my revenue model accordingly.

And so, some thirty minutes later, I felt elated as I stepped into the getaway car Claire was now driving and we made our way through the San Francisco rush hour back to Hotel Zetta for a well-earned drink or two. What a city, what a trip and what an opportunity I had to build something pioneering for the Middle Eastern market. Dr Pat in particular had inspired me with his 'can do' attitude and my proverbial cup was well and truly brimming with enthusiasm.

I slept well that night, buoyed by how lucky I was to have an opportunity to visit San Francisco and to meet such inspiring people. But now I was excited to return to the Middle East to start building something special.

As I was preparing to leave my hotel room, the phone rang. It was the reception desk, and they had Dr Pat on the line for me. Had I said something I shouldn't have? Had he just found out how many times I had contacted his girlfriend Kelly in the hope of getting access to him? Had I left my laptop in his boardroom? Why on earth was he phoning me?

'Charlie, it's Pat,' he said.

'Wow, Pat. It's great to hear from you. Is everything OK?'

'Absolutely,' he replied. 'I just really loved our meeting yesterday and I wondered if you could spare thirty minutes with me this morning before you fly out of San Francisco to have a coffee. I can be in your hotel in twenty minutes, if that works?'

Wow – Pat wasn't stringing me up for stalking his girlfriend. And he actually liked what I had said. And he was keen to come to *my* hotel to meet *me*. Dr Pat Basu. One of the most influential and successful telehealth entrepreneurs in the US. In the world. Someone whom I'd only met yesterday by lying to get into his office.

'Hell yeah. Come and see me, Pat! I'll be downstairs in the hotel café in twenty minutes.'

So, some twenty minutes later, there I was, in the ground-floor café area of Hotel Zetta in San Francisco, having coffee with Dr Pat – or 'Pat', as he asked me to call him. He loved what I had said about wanting to change how primary healthcare was accessed by low-income workers in the Middle East. He loved and respected the research I had done into him and into Doctor on Demand. He loved my hustle to get a meeting with him. And most importantly, he wanted to help.

I've always been pretty good at thinking fast, particularly in business meetings. It's a great sales skill to have, I guess. When someone takes you off guard, you need to show no surprise and drive for a conclusion that benefits you.

So when he asked what he could do, almost immediately I said, 'Well, I'd love you to be on my advisory board. I'd love to soak up everything you know about telehealth and lean on you to help me build a localised version of Doctor on Demand for the Middle East.' And there and then, during our second thirty-minute meeting on consecutive days, Pat scribbled his signature on a napkin from the Hotel Zetta café, agreeing to be an advisor to my business – and more than that, I could immediately use him on my fundraising investor deck. He'd update his LinkedIn profile to reflect his new role, and he'd commit to a weekly call, along with a trip to Dubai once my idea was a little more developed.

'I absolutely don't want any equity. Not now, or ever. I just want to help you, my friend.' A fellow entrepreneur trying to do something good in this world. What an absolute legend. A game-changer. And now a lifelong friend whose desire to help others shines bright.

As I returned to Dubai with a significantly greater understanding of the US telehealth market, the realisation dawned on me that I knew very little about the healthcare landscape in the UAE and the wider Middle East. I remembered reading that not all great ideas are turned into successful businesses, that it is fundamental for aspiring entrepreneurs to research at length the problem they are trying to solve – and thereafter develop a viable solution to this problem. Is the business idea a 'nice-to-have' or a 'must-have', and for whom are you solving the problem?

At this point I had invested considerable thought into the company name, and I believed 'Health at Hand' sounded kinder and more empathetic than Doctor4U. I was, after all, focused on building a consumer-centric business where the patient would be at the heart of every decision I made. For Health at Hand, there were several elements of Middle Eastern healthcare systems, starting with the UAE, that it would be fundamentally important to understand. Who owned the market – the consumer, the payer or the regulator? Where did the biggest problems lie – in access to healthcare or the cost of healthcare? And if I had such a brilliant idea, why was no one else doing it already?

As part of my research, I decided I needed to speak to four different healthcare stakeholder groups in the UAE to fully understand the landscape, these being:

1) the Health Authority and/or Health Regulator
2) the Insurance Companies
3) the Doctors and Clinics
4) the Patients

Each business has its own unique stakeholders. By considering who mine were, I began to determine whether Health at Hand had a shot at success or not.

I targeted the Dubai Health Authority (DHA) first. Unlike many other sectors, healthcare is highly regulated, and any healthcare business requires the endorsement and approval of a regulator to achieve a license to operate, without which it would simply not be able to launch. It was crucial for me to understand the regulator's thinking when it came to telehealth in the UAE. While much of the public sector in the UAE was famed for its red tape and its reticence when it came to digital innovation, I was pleasantly surprised by the DHA's willingness to meet and to embrace technology, motivated no doubt by the speed at which the population was growing and the consequential pressure this was having on resources.

Regulatory documents were relatively easy to access by visiting the relevant government websites, and further information could often be found in roundtable and thought-leadership pieces authored by their officers. Moreover, the DHA had participated in numerous consultations with the private sector, including with the healthcare teams of blue-chip consultancy firms such as Deloitte and Bain & Co. I was able to access many of these papers online and subsequently met with the healthcare leads at the international consultancy firm EY, as well as the team at Mubadala, a local investment and consultancy business that focused heavily on the healthcare sector.

lition, I met with legal firm Al Tamimi and Company, n regional healthcare who not only represented the DHA itself but also several international health insurance companies with regional offices. Al Tamimi's Head of Healthcare, Andrea Tithecott, was extremely generous and hugely supportive. With her help, along with my wider research, I ascertained that, though there was no specific telehealth legislation in Dubai (an explanation as to why no one else had launched a Health at Hand-type business), there was a huge desire on the part of the government to use technology to both a) increase access and b) reduce the cost of delivering primary healthcare. Immediately my name was added to DHA's Roundtable Working Group, and I was invited to the regular healthcare events hosted by the likes of EY, Deloitte and others.

When it came to meeting the actual local and international insurance companies operating in the UAE, some of my findings were eye-opening:

Firstly, it was very apparent that the insurance companies 'owned' the whole healthcare ecosystem, and it was no surprise that they were referred to as the 'payers'. With no state healthcare, international healthcare companies such as Aetna, Cigna and Canada Life had arrived in the region safe in the knowledge that a) the government were not competing with them and b) there were very few local incumbents. 70 per cent of healthcare spend was controlled by about 6–7 large payers. The big win here was that there were very few people I potentially needed to impress.

Secondly, it was clear that the insurance companies set the prices. And the cynic in me determined that, unlike my experience with meeting doctors like Pat, the payers had little concern for the well-being of their insured patients. They were motivated by one thing only – bottom-line profit. Furthermore, as populations were increasing rapidly across the whole region, the payers were finding it harder and harder to retain their margins and reach, and were crying out for low-cost, technology-enabled solutions.

Thirdly, the timing in launching a telehealth business could hardly be better. The UAE had just announced that they were to make health insurance mandatory for all residents of the country – an initiative that the rest of the region also wanted to roll out. If all employers were now required to purchase health insurance for their staff, the insurance companies would need to find a low-cost way of rolling this out and making it affordable. And furthermore, the government were mandating that the maximum amount an insurer could charge for annual healthcare insurance for a low-income, blue-collar worker was AED 160 per annum ($30–$35). How on earth was it possible to insure someone at this low a cost without a digitally enabled solution?

As my conversations developed, it seemed the real problem was not the one I had first assumed, one of access. In the Middle East it was instead a problem of cost. Health insurers were required to roll out health insurance across mass populations, but with capped pricing. Traditional methods of healthcare delivery were not going to be affordable, and a door had opened for someone to build an app whereby patients who had minor illnesses (coughs, colds, earaches) could access a doctor via their smartphone from the comfort of their own home, alleviating the need to physically visit a clinic. This also got me thinking about the possible integration of drug delivery into whatever platform I was to build. Health at Hand could, if US numbers were to be believed, treat over 70 per cent of all primary healthcare issues remotely, thus saving the consumer significant time, but more importantly for my business hopes of getting off the ground, saving the payers significant costs.

As I left the office of Christian Gregorowicz, regional CEO of global insurer Allianz's subsidiary Nextcare, I was convinced that I had nailed down the critically important problem/solution conundrum that all new aspiring entrepreneurs face. Interestingly, Christian had also expressed his interest in and understanding of telehealth: 'We love this space and are likely to build our own solution.' Rather than discourage me, this comment made me think I was on to something.

But what would the final two stakeholders, the doctors and patients, have to say about this?

Dubai is dominated by a small number of large, privately owned healthcare chains, many of which are located next to each other in the districts of Jumeirah and Umm Suqeim, along the Jumeirah Beach Road. Again, by using the likes of LinkedIn, I had made direct contact with the directors and Chief Medical Officers of many of these clinics and met with them personally, showing off my previous meetings with the regulator, the private sector payers and with the likes of Mubadala and EY. I wasn't afraid to name-drop, with more than a significant hint of poetic license, mentioning my close ties with companies such as Teladoc and MD Live in the US, and my amazing connections within the Dubai Health Authority. Many of my approaches led to meetings, but it seemed the clinics and doctors also had their own motivation to work with a company like Health at Hand. An easy win would be if we were able to increase their patient numbers, as their primary goal was seemingly 'patient acquisition'. This goal was somewhat contradictory to my own vision – I was all about reducing the need to physically see a doctor, rather than filling up doctors' waiting rooms. But a breakthrough came when I realised that telehealth could in fact help clinics acquire new patients without compromising my vision for Health at Hand. I learnt that 90 per cent of a physical clinic's patients lived within a ten-kilometre radius of the clinic's location. Through our video consultations we would allow these clinics to serve patients who lived further away, and attract new patients who were perhaps immobile due to ill health or lack of transport.

Another issue in the UAE was how doctors operated and how they were licensed. Unlike in the UK, for example, where doctors essentially own their own license to practice (and are therefore responsible for their own malpractice insurance), meaning they can essentially work for both the public and private sectors at the same time, in the UAE, a doctor's license to practice was owned by the clinic that employed them. So, an Uber-like model of attracting doctors to supplement their income by working the odd hour here and there for Health at Hand was simply not possible – not without either entering into a partnership with a doctor clinic or a complete change in how doctors were regulated and licensed. It seemed to me like more work and consultation was needed here.

I also wanted to get closer to the patients, and particularly the low-income patients of Dubai. This was the market segment that had historically not benefited from health insurance but would now require insuring, albeit at a very low cost. I would also have to find a solution to convincing patients that seeing a doctor via video was indeed as safe as seeing one face-to-face. I began swotting up on 'consumer behaviour change', reading books such as *Thinking Fast and Slow* by Daniel Kahneman. Persuading consumers to change how they accessed healthcare was not going to be done overnight, but there were case studies in the US and European markets that I could turn to.

*

Dubai's population was under a million in 2000, but by 2016 it had increased to about 2.6. While there are many countries in the Middle East with greater reserves, everything changed in 1966 when the UAE struck oil. The country's subsequent development plans could not be satisfied by the small local population, and the city of Dubai was (and still is) on a constant mission to attract foreign labour. Delivering on their growth plans required Dubai to not only attract the educated Western bankers and lawyers to work in the financial district, but there was a constant requirement to attract the low-income construction workers and labourers, the baggage handlers, the taxi drivers, those who work on the oil rigs, the gardeners and pool attendants, the shopping-mall cleaners and the housemaids. These are often referred to as the 'unseen population' of Dubai, whose hidden homes are mainly located miles into the desert, way beyond the skyscrapers, and who are bussed into the city at the crack of dawn to conduct their jobs, before returning under the cover of darkness after another twelve-hour-plus shift.

To really understand the healthcare needs of this low-income population, I knew I had to conduct some proper field research, and what better way to do this than to spend three nights in one of these labour camps in the middle of the desert. Leaning on a senior connection I had at international security company G4S, I found myself staying at an 1,800-population camp some eighteen kilometres from the bright lights of Dubai.

I was the first 'white collar worker' I had heard of who had ever contemplated such a move, but I was convinced it was a necessary step in getting under the skin of one of the demographics I wished to target.

I was to share a bunk bed with Abdullah in a cramped room of eight, with no air conditioning and a ceiling fan that worked for just two hours each day. You could spend a decade living and working in Dubai and never set eyes on such a place. But there were thousands of similar camps littered across the desert housing predominantly male workers from countries such as Pakistan, India and Bangladesh. From time to time, these communities receive international scrutiny, with reports of workers having their passports confiscated upon arrival and only having them returned every two years for a brief visit home before being ordered back to the UAE to their cramped and unhygienic dormitories.

Staying at the G4S camp was invaluable research for Health at Hand. Abdullah was a charming, devout Muslim from Kenya. His wife and three children still lived on the outskirts of Nairobi, and while his salary of $110 a week seemed incredibly low, it was considerably more than he could earn in Kenya – hence his decision to leave his family behind and seek employment in Dubai. Like many others in the Middle East, he admirably managed to send between 30–50 per cent of this salary back to his family each month. At 05:30 each morning, he and hundreds of his fellow campmates would load up on to a bus, destination Dubai, where he undertook a fourteen-hour shift in the opulent Mall of the Emirates as a security guard. Including travel time, he was lucky to return 'home' by 22:00 each day and had only one full day and two half days off each month. Fortunately for me, Abdullah was open and communicative, and once trust was established between the two of us through our mutual love of cricket, he let me in on an eye-opening failing of the UAE's healthcare system.

'Watch this,' Abdullah said in his broken English as he queued up to meet the camp doctor. In most camps, workers were afforded an individual five-minute consultation with a doctor every two months, a staggering statistic that was further motivation for me in developing a healthcare solution for low-income workers. On making it to the front of the queue, with me by his side, Abdullah feigned a stomach irritation, and without much probing from the doctor, he was given a pink form, which he was told to take to the on-site pharmacy to exchange for some prescription drugs. Asking me to accompany him to the pharmacy, Abdullah was happy to expose to me the corruption within the healthcare system.

The pink form apparently had a value to the pharmacy of around $50. On retaining Abdullah's pink ticket, the pharmacy was able to exchange the form for that $50 from either Abdullah's insurance company, his employer G4S or the government, depending on how the claim was structured. In return the pharmacy was required to give Abdullah his $50 worth of prescription drugs.

Knowing he would be able to cash this pink form for $50 of guaranteed income, the pharmacist offered Abdullah the option to exchange it for up to $40 of goods sold in the pharmacy, ranging from electric toothbrushes to sunglasses and sunscreen, rather than prescription drugs. Abdullah promptly selected a $40 hairdryer, and on taking it back to our room, he quickly uploaded an image of it on to Souq.com, a UAE e-commerce platform subsequently acquired by Amazon for $580 million. To my amazement, within less than ten minutes, Abdullah had sold his hairdryer online for $34, and it was to be collected by the buyer in person within the next four hours.

In short, Abdullah had personally made $34 from this transaction – and the pharmacist was also $25 to the good having sold a hairdryer that cost him $25 in exchange for $50. On probing deeper, it seemed this arbitrage was rife across the G4S camp, and I assumed across the hundreds of other camps in the country. I couldn't blame Abdullah: $34 was a significant amount of money to him, and if he were able to do this every two months when he visited the camp doctor, he would be able to supplement his rather measly income. While I understood that closing such a loophole would ultimately mean that migrant workers such as Abdullah would be poorer, it did get me thinking about the endemic corruption seemingly rife within the sector. I wondered how much money was lost each year to similar practices – and if technology, and perhaps Health at Hand, could play a role in alleviating this issue. A new problem had been identified through my field research, and maybe I had just the solution that would ultimately save the sector considerable amounts of money.

On further probing, it was clear that this corruption was essentially lining the pockets of the pharmacy companies, and I saw an opportunity: if I could highlight this problem to the DHA and convince them that telehealth could reduce in-person pharmacy and clinic visits by 70 per cent, Health at Hand could go some way to solving this issue. As I said earlier, find a tangible benefit for *all* your stakeholders and you are in play.

With my initial stakeholder research concluded, I had a much deeper handle on the UAE healthcare markets. The challenges were different to those which Doctor on Demand faced in the US, but by localising a similar technology stack for the UAE market, I might just be able to come up with a solution to some of the sector's most pressing problems.

KEY TAKEAWAYS

- **Solve a real problem.** In the case study of Health at Hand, I analysed our four main stakeholders and determined how our solution might benefit them all:

  1) For the DHA, our solution would assist them in rolling out cost-efficient health insurance across mass populations and help them alleviate some of the endemic corruption in the healthcare sector.
  2) For the insurers, we could drive cost containment by alleviating the need for hundreds of patients to visit a doctor in person.
  3) For doctors and clinics, we would enable them to acquire patients who lived far from their clinic or who were unable to visit them in person, thus helping their patient-acquisition strategy without compromising our own vision.
  4) For patients, we could deliver convenience and a twenty-four-hour service.

- **Research the hell out of your idea.** There may well be a reason why no one else has launched a similar business in your target market. Chat to experts, question, probe and test your hypothesis on the market.
- **Have faith in your ability.** You've had the tenacity to get this far, and you are just as good as the next person.
- **Copy-cat businesses are often the most successful.** You don't need to reinvent the wheel. There is a reason why telehealth was performing well in the US – essentially it was a bloody good idea that hadn't yet reached the Middle East. Don't be afraid to copy best practices from other companies and markets and then localise a solution for your target market.

3

BUILD FOR SUCCESS

*'Shoot for the moon. Even if you miss,
you'll land among the stars.'*

NORMAN VINCENT PEALE, AUTHOR OF
THE POWER OF POSITIVE THINKING

Two attributes of a good entrepreneur are understanding where they excel and, equally important, the areas in which they are lacking the skills their business requires to succeed. Health at Hand was not necessarily going to be a straightforward business to build, and I had been warned that, given the ambitions I had for the company, we would require a 'rich tech stack'. I determined that in the early months of the business I would need to focus my time on three key areas, these being technology, supply (essentially doctors) and demand (patients). I visualised the business as a triangle with each of these focus areas taking up their own corner, with functions such as finance, legal and human resources occupying the space in the middle.

Bizarrely, I was not necessarily either skilled or experienced in any of the three corners of the Health at Hand triangle, but I backed myself as a leader who could bring together the right experts, a puppeteer of sorts. With my energy and determination, I was confident that I could quickly assemble a high-performing team on a mission to solve the problems I had analysed in the Middle East's primary-healthcare sector.

I subsequently began my search to onboard an expert in each of these areas of focus. I was determined to put together a dream team able to support the initial build-phase of the business and determined to aim high in terms of the calibre of individual I approached. Without being able to pay this proposed team anything until we raised finance – but wanting to lean heavily on their time – I decided to give them all some equity in the business from day one. One of my core beliefs, long before Health at Hand was even conceived, was that if I ever launched my own business, the financial success would be shared by everyone involved. This was my opportunity to put that principle into action. One of the greatest advantages of building your own company is the ability to shape it according to your own values and vision. Drawing from years of experience as an employee, I had the chance to carry forward the best practices I had encountered, while also addressing the areas I had often found frustrating – whether it was limited holiday days, rigid dress codes, inflexible hours or insufficient benefits. I was determined to create the kind of workplace I had always wanted to be a part of.

At this time, I frequently used the phrase 'Build for Success', and this extended to how I would ultimately set up Health at Hand as a legal entity. I had read so many stories of startups failing because they had not set their business up correctly, and often despite having what I considered brilliant ideas at their core. I will be forever grateful that I listened to them, drawing up a set of globally recognised, professional legal documents that meant there was no ambiguity when I ultimately came to sell the company.

Numerous people in my network warned me:

a) to trust no one
b) to ensure formal legal contracts were in place (especially where friends and family were concerned) and
c) to structure the business professionally from the get-go.

I was fortunate to know several young, savvy lawyers based in Dubai, all with international experience – and crucially, experience in establishing corporate entities for startup companies like mine. Had I not had these personal connections, I would no doubt have used resources like LinkedIn to research such experts.

For entrepreneurs who more generally speaking may not have such a well-established network, I would recommend starting by tapping into local workshops, or meetups where you can connect with industry professionals. Often the sector you are working in will have an industry body that you can join, and you will find a huge number of industry-specific forums online, which will help you to identify and reach out to potential mentors and advisors. Building relationships can take time, but by being proactive and genuine in your outreach, as I hope I was with the likes of Dr Pat, you can gradually expand your own network and gain valuable insights and support.

As a business we were what you would call 'boot-strapped'. I was personally funding the costs from my own savings until a time that we managed to raise money, and I was willing to part with a few thousand dollars to take some professional legal advice to avoid any problems further down the line. On this expert advice, I ultimately found myself establishing a corporate entity in the Dubai Multi Commodities Centre (DMCC), a 'freezone' that afforded early-stage businesses tax and licensing benefits. Importantly, above this company I established a British Virgin Island (BVI) company which acted as the holding company for Health at Hand DMCC, as its 100 per cent owner. This structure was a well-trodden path in the Middle East, allowing funds to be held tax efficiently at the BVI level and only drawn down into the Dubai entity as and when required. I learnt that non-Middle Eastern investors were reassured by this structure and would rather own a stake in a BVI entity than direct shares in a company established in the Middle East. There was still considerable mistrust in the banking systems of the region, and this was one way to negate any investor concerns.

The additional benefit of establishing a BVI entity was that they came with an incredibly comprehensive set of legal documents, including internationally recognised Shareholder Agreements and Memorandum and Articles of Association, all based on UK law. Such a structure required Health at Hand to file an annual return, hugely reassuring to incoming investors and providing integrity regarding how the money was being deployed.

In my quest to 'Build for Success' I wanted my three initial hires to be brilliant in their own fields of expertise. Just as I aimed very high in persuading Dr Pat to support the business, I knew that a strong initial team would not only allow me to build Health at Hand at speed but would serve to impress and reassure any potential investors.

I debated at length what the right level of equity was to give away to these core members of the business. Too little and the team wouldn't be sufficiently motivated to help me, particularly given they were to only 'moonlight' with Health at Hand in the early days, keeping their current jobs until such a time that the business could afford to pay them. On the flip side, if I gave up too much equity, I was fearful that my own equity stake would be quickly diluted and I would no longer control the business. I concluded that I'd be comfortable in collectively offering around 10 per cent equity to these three hires, and true to my 'Build for Success' mantra, each of the individuals would immediately sign an official Shareholder Agreement to reflect this decision, ensuring there would be no conflict further down the line. Furthermore, within each legal contract I included a prescriptive list of 'deliverables' – if they failed to execute on them, the company (essentially myself) could clawback some of this equity allocation. This allowed me to 'de-risk' my generosity if they did not perform.

Amy was a great friend. She had been at university in the UK with my wife Claire, was bright and energetic, had a phenomenal work ethic and wasn't afraid to speak her mind. I obviously considered the 'is it wise to work with friends?' conundrum and determined that bringing Amy on board would not compromise our friendship – and, furthermore, I was also confident that our closeness would not dampen Amy's opinionated and contrarian mindset. It was my belief that it would be a huge mistake to surround myself purely with 'yes-people', and I was determined to build a culture that encouraged debate and the differing of opinions.

Amy was an incredibly skilled marketeer, at the time working in project management and marketing for the Arab Radio Network, and was adept at developing and implementing strategic initiatives. I was incredibly fond of her. She was great at what she did, and I believed she'd be a huge asset to Health at Hand. I also knew she'd have my back. Amy's expertise would allow her to lead on the 'demand' corner of the triangle, conducting extensive market research into patients and digging deep into the consumer-behaviour-change challenge associated with delivering remote healthcare. As a mother herself, she also represented what we anticipated being one of our main patient personas: time-poor, middle-class expatriate mothers who had access to a comprehensive family-healthcare insurance plan via their employer.

Jenna was a hugely capable and bubbly doctor from the UK who had been living in Dubai for several years with her lawyer husband. Jenna's smile and personality entered the room before she did, and it seemed she was loved by all who worked with her. She had an infectious character, coupled with a capacity to juggle multiple roles that allowed her to work part time across several different private-sector healthcare companies. Jenna also came highly recommended by Mark Adams, an experienced healthcare CEO, Chair and non-executive director, who I respected hugely and who I met with frequently in these early days to brainstorm about the sector. Jenna was a perfect addition to the team to head up the 'supply' corner of the triangle, exploring how we could attract doctors to work for Health at Hand while at the same time commencing our work on clinical pathways, the 'what we treat' sections of our documentation and looking into any licensing and malpractice considerations.

Aftab was from a completely different background to Amy and Jenna, which perfectly aligned with my desire to encourage diversity of people and thought. In his mid-twenties, Aftab was an ambitious project manager with a Bachelor of Science degree from the

National University of Computer Sciences in his home city of Karachi, Pakistan. I met Aftab through my connections with a local technology accelerator called Astrolabs, which fosters relationships between startup companies and the wider technology ecosystem. At the time, Aftab was working for the Government of Qatar in the Ministry of Information and Communication Technology, but he was interested in getting involved in a more entrepreneurial business. Given my obvious lack of technological expertise, Aftab was a crucial member of the initial team, heading up the 'technology' corner of the triangle, translating my often overly optimistic dreams for Health at Hand's technology platform into reality. He knew what was possible and wasn't afraid to tell me.

I also wanted to find a role for my great and trusted friend, Nadim. He and I had been at university together some years before, both studying Business Management at the University of London, with Nadim moving from the UK to Dubai five or six years ahead of me. Nadim was great fun, and someone whom I knew would always offer me fair and constructive advice. Not only was he far more knowledgeable about technology than I was – his fifteen years in leadership roles at Cisco Systems easily outweighed my equivalent time in banking – but he was also a year or two ahead of Health at Hand in his own entrepreneurial journey. Nadim was building a mobile-payment business for Middle Eastern retailers called Beam Wallet, giving him invaluable experience in navigating the challenges of a startup in the region. Thankfully, Nadim had both the ability and appetite to share his own experiences as an entrepreneur – both good and bad – and without thinking for too long on it, I granted Nadim a similar equity percentage as the rest of the team and brought him on to the board of Health at Hand alongside myself.

At the same time, I was keen that we built a brilliant brand for the business. Perception is everything, and I wanted to ensure we had some solid investor documentation in place, knowing that the more professional the business looked, and the more investor questions I could pre-empt within our marketing literature, the greater the chance we had of raising capital at a high valuation.

To build out the brand I looked no further than my friend Gaurav, who ran a hugely successful marketing and branding agency called Insignia. Despite much of his work being focused on the hotel and hospitality sector, I was not put off. Gaurav was a wonderful wordsmith and storyteller with a huge team behind him. I had a few years earlier referred some business to Gaurav from a hotelier I knew in the Maldives and having not asked Gaurav for a referral fee at the time, I knew I had some credit in the bank with him. Gaurav was happy to build a comprehensive brand bible for the business in return for a modest equity stake in Health at Hand. He also came up with our name, quickly dismissing Doctor4U as an option, and our associated logo – both of which survive today.

So, there we had it. A dream team cleverly assembled without me spending any of my own money, but one that I believed would:

a) help advance the development of the business
b) impress potential investors, and
c) only see me give up a modest percentage of the company's equity.

Over the next few weeks and months, the dream team met as frequently as we could in the coffee shops and hotel foyers of Dubai, stealing an hour here and an hour there during public holidays, weekends and lunch breaks. Each member of the team pulled their own weight, and we soon managed to find comprehensive answers to the various hypotheses and assumptions which we had challenged ourselves with.

It was at this point that I also persuaded Pat to visit Dubai from San Francisco for three days, bringing his girlfriend Kelly with him on their first ever trip to the region. Given we hadn't yet raised any funding, I knew that any trip would have to be paid for by myself, but I was willing to do so given the amazing insights that Pat could potentially give us into the workings of a well-oiled telehealth company.

Keen to roll out the red carpet for Pat, I asked Rasica's husband to collect Pat and Kelly in my car from Dubai International Airport and paid for Pat and his wife to stay in one of my favourite local hotels, the Jumeirah Beach Hotel (JBH), some five minutes from where I lived in Umm Suqeim. While there were numerous more expensive options in Dubai, as the name suggests, the JBH was right on the beach, and famous for its hospitality and warm welcome – it would provide Pat and Kelly with an incredibly soft landing after their twenty hours of travel.

Claire and I dressed up that evening and met Pat and Kelly for supper in the trendy Japanese restaurant Zuma, located in the Dubai International Finance Centre where many of the city's finest restaurants resided and its working professionals congregated. Pat and Kelly were both incredible company and the four of us got on brilliantly. Sharing our love of politics, sport and travel – aside from our mutual interest in telehealth – we recalled tales of our childhoods and to our delight Claire and I learnt that Pat and Kelly had recently become engaged. I could already sense that a special friendship was building.

Over the subsequent three days, I worked Pat hard in numerous workshops with the Health at Hand team. We trawled through the detailed financial model I had built, discussed the valuation of the business and pondered over client onboarding and utilisation rates, while I learnt about which ailments telehealth had thus far treated most successfully and came to understand the metrics with which Pat managed his own business, Doctor on Demand. Most importantly, I learnt about clinical pathways, the crucial role of a Chief Medical Officer and the importance of malpractice insurance.

On Pat's final evening I rolled him out to meet some of my newly acquired contacts in the healthcare sector, including David Taylor, the Managing Director of Medacs – the Middle East's largest and most successful doctor recruitment firm – a representative from the Dubai Health Authority, a number of health insurance professionals and the CEO of the region's largest pharmaceutical chain, Aster Pharmacy.

When Pat left the following morning, we really did feel buoyed by the opportunity he had given us. As a team we had squeezed as much information out of him as we could have hoped. I sensed that he too felt there was a great opportunity for us to build something special in the region, and his genuine enthusiasm for Health at Hand had been a huge tonic.

Much of the work we did in the following days was to determine what our technology platform needed to look like to deliver on our vision. It is here that Aftab came into his own.

I had already learnt a considerable amount from Nadim about not accumulating technology debt, the consequences of building quick and dirty technology solutions over robust and efficient ones that you could use in years to come. Accumulating technology debt – also known as technical debt – can present significant dangers for a business, particularly over the long term. While technical debt allows companies to push out solutions quickly, bypassing optimal or long-term approaches, the costs can compound and cause issues at scale.

To avoid this, it was important to understand what we wanted our technology platform to look like in five years' time and work backwards from there. In a technology startup, a Minimum Viable Product (MVP) is the simplest version of a product that includes only its core features – just enough to meet the needs of early adopters and gather feedback. The goal is to quickly test assumptions, validate market demand and then iterate with minimal investment based on user insights. MVPs are crucial because they allow startups to avoid wasted resources on unnecessary features, reduce the time to market and mitigate risk by learning what works (or doesn't) before committing to full-scale development. This lean approach fosters agility and ensures that the product evolves based on real user needs. We needed an MVP that was robust enough and had enough features to attract our early adopters, without costing the earth. We then needed to stack rank, when we would build out the additional features and expand the time, team and money it would take to do so. Aftab was invaluable in this process, and our five-year product roadmap was an essential piece of our jigsaw.

It became clear that Aftab was more of a Technical Product Manager than a pure Product Manager, the difference being that he had knowledge of computer science, software development and engineering. He had dabbled in coding, without being an engineer per se, and was skilled in determining the 'how' we were going to build our solution as opposed to just the 'what' and the 'why', which were essentially driven by myself.

Importantly, not having an engineering background myself, Aftab could also keep our engineers honest. An analogy I often use is taking your car to a mechanic, only to be told you need a new exhaust. Most of us aren't equipped to question the mechanic's expertise, as we lack the technical knowledge they possess. This creates a dilemma: we're forced to trust their diagnosis, assuming it to be both accurate and honest, before handing over our money. I really didn't want us to have the wool pulled over our eyes by any third-party suppliers or engineers we were to use either then or in the future. It was incredibly important to me to have at least one team member who really understood how long a product should reasonably take to build, how many hours or spring cycles it should take to build a specific feature and how much all of this should cost. Many technology startup businesses fall over when they are led by a non-technical founder or CEO. They are susceptible to overpaying for certain features, for wasting time in the build process and for accumulating technology debt.

In this sense, Aftab was my chief lieutenant, and he played a vital role in ensuring that we used our money and time wisely. Through hours and hours of workshopping, Aftab was able to deliver a comprehensive product strategy and technology roadmap for the business including an in-depth analysis of which expert engineers we needed to hire and when, alongside a detailed cost analysis that would feed into our financial projections.

It was clear that we would initially require a diverse team of iOS and Android specialists, a couple of back-end engineers and at least one quality-assurance lead. Given I was unwilling to give up too much equity in our initial upcoming fund raise, and the fact that my bootstrapping of the business was becoming rather expensive, Aftab and I determined that the most cost-efficient route to achieve our technology ambitions was via an outsourced model, essentially paying a third-party technology agency to provide the engineering team expertise and thereby avoiding the cost of hiring engineers ourselves. This model was a well-trodden path for early-stage technology businesses and would allow us to save on the likes of recruitment fees and staff visas.

This approach was not without its risks. I was particularly concerned that outsourced engineers might not feel fully invested in the project, since they were not full-time Health at Hand employees. We also recognised the potential impact on company culture from having a mix of full-time and outsourced team members. However, after weighing the pros and cons, Aftab and I agreed that this model was the best option in the company's early stages. We were confident that we could navigate the cultural challenges, and given our limited finances at the time, it was a practical necessity. We did, however, make a commitment that as the business grew, we would aim to gradually bring engineering talent in-house.

With the help of several generous people from Astrolabs, Aftab and I interviewed a variety of third-party engineering companies and decided to hire the Dubai-based company Mokus, run by a talented Syrian called Rima. Mokus employed numerous engineers, primarily located in Dubai and across Eastern Europe, including Rima's girlfriend who was equally talented and acted as her number two. Over the subsequent months I spent many hours in Rima's cramped apartment in Motor City, fuelled by endless cups of tea and biscuits as we built out the MVP.

It was not just money that motivated my desire to make Health at Hand a success. I would be lying if I said that making a financial gain from the business was not important to me, but I was also driven by the purpose of the business. Looking back to when I discovered that Rasica was not afforded the same healthcare benefits as myself,

I was still really invested in making a difference and solving the inequality clearly present in the Dubai healthcare sector. To this end, I thought long and hard about the mission, vision and values of the business and read numerous books and articles on purpose versus profit. It was important to me that the team were aware of my desire to build a business with purpose at its heart – and I was also keen that they all bought into our values. It was also something I wanted to come across in our investment documentations, too. In time, I wanted to attract strategic and supportive investors – not just money for the sake of it – and I made it very clear that as a business we were on a mission to make primary healthcare more accessible and affordable – as well as hopefully making significant returns for all our shareholders.

After much deliberation, and in consultation with the team, we encapsulated our mission, vision and values in one easy-to-articulate statement:

> Health at Hand aims to bring the highest standard of healthcare to everyone, wherever and whenever it is needed the most. Convenient and trusted, we aim to remove the difficulties commonly experienced when visiting the doctor. This is the future of healthcare.

We now had the not insignificant task of raising money from the investment community. I put together a comprehensive data room to support our efforts, including a detailed financial model, outlining our forward-looking growth projections, alongside a beautifully crafted investment presentation considerately put together by Gaurav and his team of expert designers.

*

There are several important considerations for founders when raising a first round of seed capital, and it was important that I considered each before I went out to the market with cap in hand:

1. Valuation and Equity Dilution

Founders must carefully determine how much their company is worth at this early stage. A lower valuation might attract investors but will result in giving away more equity. I was also keen that my own personal stake in the business was not diluted so much as to demotivate me going forward. It was a fine balancing act between attracting investors with my valuation but not giving too much away.

2. Use of Funds

It was important that I clearly defined how the seed capital would be used, and detail what percentage I planned to spend on the likes of product development, hiring, marketing and scaling operations. Investors always want to see a strategic plan for the capital spend to understand how it will fuel growth.

3. Terms of Investment

For me it was important that any external investment was structured in the right way. In many early-stage companies, investors can ask for what is called 'liquidation preferences' or 'anti-dilution clauses', effectively de-risking their investments if the company doesn't grow at the pace they want. A liquidation preference is a clause that guarantees that investors are paid back before common shareholders (such as founders or employees) in the event of a liquidation, sale or bankruptcy. It outlines how much investors will receive, typically their initial investment or a multiple of it, before any remaining proceeds are distributed. I was of course keen to ensure that my own personal stake was protected and managed to negotiate hard so that each incoming investor would pay simple cash for equity, with no preferential terms on the exit of the business over and above my own shares or anyone else's.

4. Traction and Proof of Concept

Having a working prototype was certainly an attraction of Health at Hand as we raised our first investment round. We were more than just a team and an idea when we first approached investors, and I was delighted that we had something tangible to show investors, albeit an MVP that was yet to be fully tested by real patients and doctors.

5. Runway and Future Rounds

It is important for founders that they seek to raise enough capital to provide a sufficiently long runway to allow them to increase the valuation of their business. The last thing I wanted to do was go back out to the market within twelve months and seek more funding. A second round this early is not only a distraction for founders but often doesn't give them enough time to turn that initial investment into a significantly higher valuation. You certainly want to avoid what the market calls a 'down-round', where you are effectively raising capital again but at a lower valuation than you did the first time. In the case of Health at Hand, I was ideally looking to give the business twenty-four months of runway to advance it to a stage where we could raise funds again at a much higher valuation.

In determining the valuation of the business, I leaned on my sixteen years in banking. Financial models and valuation metrics were something I was very comfortable with. While the valuation of a business at such an early stage is not a perfect science – it's just a guide to how much someone might be prepared to pay for shares in your business, given you haven't built anything yet – it was important to me to put some science behind the valuation rather than just throwing out random and poorly researched figures to investors. This, I believed, would give me more credibility in investor meetings.

I assisted prospective investors in their due diligence by developing comprehensive five-year growth projections within my financial model, incorporating conservative, moderate, and aggressive growth assumptions so that they could scenario-plan. Additionally, I conducted thorough research on the valuations of comparable businesses that had recently secured funding. And using the growth projections in our financial model, I applied various common valuation methods to Health at Hand, including the Price-to-Earnings (P/E) multiple – typically used by more mature businesses, but still valuable context for our capital raise.

My financial model told me that we needed to raise about $1 million of investment to launch and build out our MVP, which from my calculations afforded us about twenty-four months of runway. Taking an average of all the numbers I had crunched for the business, the valuation I attributed to Health at Hand came out at circa $3 million.

A $1 million equity raise for a business valued at $3 million is referred to as either a '$3 million pre-money valuation' or a '$4 million post-money valuation'. The inevitable equity dilution for all current shareholders could be arrived at by dividing the investment amount by the post-money valuation, in this case $1 million divided by $4 million for a 25 per cent dilution. In my case, if successful in raising $1 million at this valuation, I would see my equity stake reduce from 89 per cent to 66.75 per cent. I was happy with this. I'd still be over the important 50 per cent mark, ensuring I'd retain control of the business, and I'd own 66.57 per cent of a business with $1 million in the bank. Some entrepreneurs struggle to understand the fundamental principle that owning a smaller stake in a more valuable business is more advantageous than holding a larger stake in a less valuable one.

It was now over to me to ensure the business was indeed worth $3 million based on the limited amount of work we had done.

The Bin Laden headquarters in Jeddah was not as intimidating as you would imagine. Jeddah is a pleasant enough coastal city located along the Red Sea in the Hejaz region of the Kingdom of Saudi Arabia, famed among other things for being a travel hub on the journey to the holy city of Mecca.

Boasting the second largest seaport in the Middle East, after Dubai's Port of Jebel Ali, Jeddah had more charm than the other Saudi cities I had visited in the country, including Riyadh, the capital, and Dammam in the east, the centre of the Saudi oil industry.

Taking a taxi from my modest Jeddah city hotel, I approached a small security hut at the entrance of what was a huge, opulent mansion, and on producing my passport, I was ushered through the gates and dropped under a marble arch to be greeted by an incredibly well-dressed and polite Jordanian man called Ahmed.

Having read the brilliant book *The Bin Ladens, an Arabian Family in the American Century* by Steve Coll, it came as no surprise that the Bin Laden family were comfortable employing Jordanians, with both countries boasting Sunni monarchies and enjoying cordial relations.

While the Bin Laden family name will be forever inextricably connected with and tainted by the atrocities of 9/11, the wider family were still one of huge wealth and reputation in the 'Kingdom', controlling the family construction firm, the Saudi Binladin Group.

The Saudi Binladin Group were reputedly worth well in excess of $10 billion and made the Bin Ladens reportedly one of the five wealthiest families in the Kingdom. In my search for investment for Health at Hand, I was willing to conduct as many investment meetings as possible, and the wealthy regional families were a good starting point. While their core business was construction, like multiple other family-owned conglomerates in the region, the Saudi Binladin Group's vast wealth allowed them to also invest more modest amounts of money (still in the millions) into other sectors. I had been introduced by email to one member of the family, supposedly interested in early-stage technology investments, with a specific focus on the education and healthcare sectors.

Ahmed ushered me through a seemingly endless labyrinth of corridors and stairs until I was led into a vast, opulent room adorned with ornate cornicing and gold-coloured fabric sofas along all four walls. Such a space, commonly known as a *majlis* in the Arab world, is a meeting room to entertain visitors, and while I had experienced many *majlises* in my years living in the region, never had I witnessed one of such extravagance. 'The next person you will see is Mohammed bin Laden,' announced Ahmed, 'and as soon as you see my face again, your meeting will officially be over.' On saying this, he departed stage left, shutting the door behind him and leaving me to wait it out for Bin Laden's arrival.

Such an introduction may seem out of place in other parts of the world, but having lived in the Middle East for several years, I was used to similar situations. It took a braver man than me to turn down a meeting with a prominent local family member or a member of a regional ruling family, even if on occasion it was impossible to determine who exactly it was you were meeting with in advance. While family trees are often available online, the many children born into each family makes the task of researching individuals incredibly difficult.

This meeting was slightly different to many I had had before in that I was meeting a particularly senior member of the family, and someone who friends had confirmed was both incredibly wealthy and an active investor in technology businesses.

Mohammed made me wait for about thirty minutes before he entered the room, allowing me sufficient time to take numerous photos of his grand *majlis*. When he did finally appear, it was obvious that he was a man of considerable charm. He was surprisingly well-read when it came to telehealth and its application in primary healthcare. The early signs were positive, and on the spot, as our meeting came to a conclusion, he phoned his venture-capital investment director, based in London's Mayfair, and then asked me to arrange a flight to London for me to meet with him personally.

Fundraising requires the kissing of many frogs, and while the Bin Ladens' investment into Health at Hand ultimately did not materialise – perhaps a blessing in disguise given their family's international reputation – they were another name I could drop into subsequent investor meetings in the region. Investors are often like sheep: find the first one and others will be reassured to follow!

In the case of Health at Hand, for this first investment raise I didn't need to look much further than my close network of contacts, and I quickly succeeded in raising the £1 million with relative ease using my personal black book I had accumulated during my banking days. While I acknowledge that it is not always as easy as this to raise money, I had been conscious throughout my career to not burn bridges with people, be they colleagues, clients or business contacts. Twelve investors in total committed between $50,000 and $200,000 each. While none of these individual investors were officially friends or family, more acquaintances of mine, we did indeed call this our 'Friends and Family Investment Round', as is quite common with other startup companies.

Within days the money arrived in the Health at Hand bank account, and we were up and running.

KEY TAKEAWAYS

- **Hire well – and aim high.** You'll never know if you don't at least try, so attempt to hire the very best of your network. I was very lucky that everyone I approached to be part of my initial leadership team was sufficiently persuaded to help based on the equity I offered them.
- **Know your weaknesses.** When determining what skills and experience your business needs, be self-reflective. And then be honest with yourself – which of these skills do you possess, and which do you need to hire in?
- **Surround yourself with brighter people than yourself.** The founder doesn't have to be the smartest person in the room, but you do need the ability to bring together and motivate a high-performing team.
- **Be careful how you structure your investment round.** Don't willingly offer up the likes of liquidation preferences. Make sure you build a detailed investor deck which proactively tries to anticipate and answer the questions you will be asked. And make sure everything is documented legally from the get-go. You never know what might happen further down the line.

4
CULTURE IS EVERYTHING

'Hire great people and give them the freedom to be awesome'

ANDREW MASON, FOUNDER OF GROUPON

One of the huge advantages of building your own business is that you can do it your way. Unlike entrepreneurs who start companies early in their career, I had the benefit of sixteen years of corporate experience before I founded Health at Hand, and more than that, it was diverse experience.

My working life started at Morgan Stanley in Canary Wharf, London, where I gained a place on their graduate trainee scheme straight out of university. I was moved from department to department to understand the workings of a large US bank and was initially thrust on to the trading floor, at the time the largest in Europe. It was everything I had expected and wanted. A million-miles-an-hour, fast-paced environment buzzing with testosterone.

I arrived early on my first day and was astounded by the sheer size of the office and the facilities available, ranging from an in-house doctor and dentist to three canteens, a high-tech gym for executives and another for non-executives. I quickly realised that these facilities were designed to keep us all in the office with no excuses for arriving late or leaving early. More than this, the perception there, and at other US banks, was that the more hours you were at your desk for, the better you were at your job – a totally misguided argument, which I completely challenged when building out Health at Hand's culture some years later.

At Morgan Stanley, if you were still in the office at 9 pm, they would pay for you to take a taxi home and for you to have a takeaway of your choice delivered. My colleagues and I regularly pushed these boundaries, and could be seen in the pubs and bars of Canary Wharf from 7–9 pm a couple of times a week, before we returned to the office to claim our free ride home and pizza!

On my first day I 'shadowed' one of the few female traders on the floor. I recall how at 7 am she telephoned her daughter to apologise for not being at home to make her breakfast or take her to school – and then again at 8 pm to apologise for not being there to tuck her into bed. This same pattern continued day after day, and I questioned whether the money she was earning was really worth such a sacrifice.

On days when my working hours needed to align with the Asian stock markets being open, I was required to be at my desk throughout the night. During these night shifts, as soon as the bell rang for the opening of the Hong Kong stock market you could feel the buzz of anticipation for the wild few hours that lay ahead. This was some years before the movie *The Wolf of Wall Street* hit our screens, but it really was like a scene from the film. I distinctly remember one of the traders losing a significant amount of money on a trade later that morning and watching him punch straight through his computer screen, lacerating his hand and arm in the process.

My fellow graduates and I were shocked and excited in equal measure at the pace of the environment. On one particularly challenging day I pulled an all-nighter: upon finishing my initial shift at 4 am, I was driven home in a taxi that waited outside my apartment for thirty minutes while I took a quick shower and changed my shirt – before taking me straight back to the office for another twelve-hour shift.

While the environment was undoubtedly exhilarating, I soon realised that I couldn't keep up with the demands of such a bank: the relentlessly long hours, the unwavering commitment and being surrounded by people who were evidently more driven and brighter than myself. Within eighteen months I sought refuge in the relative calm of private banking and spent the next five years working for Kleinwort Benson (KB) in the City of London. KB were a typical old-school private bank, managing money for British millionaires and their families, a combination of landed gentry and newly successful entrepreneurs. Private banking in those days was an incredibly fun place to be, particularly because it was before the risk and compliance teams within the banking sector swelled in size. The likes of Nick Leeson, who had single-handedly brought down Barings Bank through his fraudulent derivatives trades some years earlier, didn't help, but we still had the freedom to perform numerous roles within the bank.

I had an interesting and diverse role. I was part trader, trusted with tapping multi-million-pound deals into our trading systems and calculating the related currency hedge, with which we protected all our positions. I was part equity analyst and fund manager, responsible for managing our in-house Asian equity fund, which at times held only twelve stocks – an incredibly risky and concentrated strategy that would be unthinkable in today's market due to its lack of diversity. And I was part relationship manager, which meant I could wine and dine many of our high-profile high-net-worth clients in the wood-panelled rooms of our adjacent investment banking office – all while walking them through how we were growing their assets using our skill and guile. My clients at the time included three FTSE100 chairmen, the owner of a Formula One racing team and a member of the British Royal Family.

Admittedly it was not as fast and furious an environment as Morgan Stanley. Our working hours were more conventional, and the atmosphere was certainly more laid back. I distinctly remember being able to smoke in the office and having an ashtray and lighter permanently stationed in the top drawer of my desk. Our trading screens were often taken over by coverage of Wimbledon or some golf tournament or other, however, on 9/11, I recall standing open-mouthed next to my colleagues as we witnessed the second plane fly into the South Tower on those same screens.

In my capacity as a fund manager, I had four banks and research houses brokering stocks to me, these being Deutsche Bank, Credit Suisse and two boutique broking houses called Kim Eng Securities and CLSA. Their role was to try and convince me of which Asian companies to buy for the KB Asian equity fund. We received their research for free, the quid pro being that if I took their advice and acted on their recommendations, I would execute my trades through them, earning them commission. So, as a 'buy-side' banker myself, the 'sell-side' firms sought my business, putting me in the enviable position of being in demand. Consequently, I was taken for a wine-fuelled lunch each Friday at a different Michelin-starred City of London restaurant by one of these four companies, or others who wanted my business. On top of this, all-expenses-paid days out were a regular occurrence, including frequent pheasant shooting days alongside trips to Royal Ascot, Wimbledon and Twickenham.

My boss was an inspiring woman called Jo Johnson, ten years older than me and someone I learnt a huge amount from. Jo was great fun and did only as much work as was required, but at the same time was a brilliant private banker. She had an amazing knack for researching a client's portfolio just minutes before they entered the office and then being able to instantly recite exactly what British Airways' share price had done that month, or why we were weighting the consumer-goods sector over oil and gas in their portfolio. I too was able to lean on my tried and trusted exam technique of last-minute cramming and a good short-term memory.

Jo's laid-back approach to banking was emphasised by the fact she had a pile of high heels under her desk that she'd only wear when her clients came in for a meeting, replacing the trainers she had worn for her daily commute. This was long before the post-pandemic work-from-home culture, and I learnt an immeasurable amount from being around bankers more senior than myself, including Jo, and listening to how they interacted on client calls and amongst each other.

Once I'd passed the required exams to manage client money, Jo and I would visit our clients' country estates together, as well as the boardrooms of some of the City's most successful businessmen and women, as we looked to swell the investment portfolios of the already rich.

Despite my client roster being dominated by what you would call 'old money', my overwhelmingly favourite client was a great chap called Paul Wallace who was from Essex, a UK county renowned more for wheeler-dealer types than landed gentry. Paul grew up on a pig farm and, learning that they were something of a delicacy in China, he decided to take his father's discarded pigs trotters, vacuum pack them and send them to Asia, making him millions in the process. Whereas other clients came into the office for their half yearly review (and a four-course lunch, complete with pudding wine and a comprehensive cheese board) in their Rolls-Royces or Aston Martins, Paul arrived in a yellow Lamborghini adorned with pink neon lights on the underside of the car. He was great company and an entrepreneur in the real sense of the word, being someone who had come from nothing and through his own hard graft afforded himself the lifestyle he had dreamt of growing up.

The diversity of both the work and the clients that I had at KB made for a hugely enjoyable few years, but I also loved the incredibly sociable side of private banking, which saw myself and my colleagues regularly sample the many wine bars and pubs in the City of London, making some lifelong friendships along the way. The contrast between KB and my previous role at Morgan Stanley was stark, with KB's culture far better suited to my personal desire for a healthy work-life balance.

In the evenings I would ride my moped along the Embankment back to my flat in Fulham, and frequent Joe's Brasserie on Wandsworth Bridge Road, which my friends and I treated a bit like our own Central Perk from *Friends*. Without needing to announce our plans, I could turn up on any night of the week and anywhere between five and ten of my close friends would be sat in the same seats as the night before, sharing a bottle of wine or three.

Life was pretty bloody brilliant, and for the first time I had some disposable income to enjoy myself, having paid back my student debt but without the financial burden of a hefty mortgage or children. I had saved enough to buy a cosy two-bedroom flat less than five minutes' walk from Joe's Brasserie, and my friends and I enjoyed all that Fulham and Chelsea had to offer in terms of bars, restaurants and night clubs.

There was, however, something missing. I had this great desire to live and work abroad, perhaps inspired by the independence I had gained from boarding school, my brother's love of travel and the hugely enjoyable gap year I had taken between school and university when I had travelled to Singapore and Malaysia en route to Australia where I taught sport at Sydney Grammar School. After four or five years in London, I began exploring job opportunities abroad with no particular destination in mind.

Following my gap year I had travelled across Europe and to far-flung locations such as Sri Lanka, Cuba and Thailand, and immediately before my time at KB I had hitch-hiked across nine African countries (from Nairobi in Kenya to Johannesburg in South Africa), accompanied by three of my closest friends. I had a taste for new countries and cultures but craved actually living somewhere other than England and immersing myself into a new culture.

It was during this period that I met Claire on a blind date, in Joe's Brasserie of course, and was honest with her from the outset that I was looking for overseas jobs and that I would love her to join me on the adventure if she wished to.

Overseas jobs rarely land in your lap, and I am huge believer that you make your own luck in life. So many of my friends subsequently told me that they would have loved to work overseas but 'the opportunity never came their way'. Well, in my mind, you've got to make these opportunities yourself and I worked hard at sourcing banking roles in the likes of Switzerland, South Africa and the US before being offered a dream private banking role with HSBC in Hong Kong. Claire and I jumped at the opportunity, and knowing a small number of friends who had made the same move a few months ahead of us, we were excited to begin our new adventure together in Asia.

Arriving in the hustle and bustle of Hong Kong is something I will never forget, and moving overseas remains one of the best decisions Claire and I have ever made. We started our life in an HSBC-paid-for flat in trendy SoHo before moving to an exciting (yet small) one-bedroom flat just off Hong Kong's famous escalator – a walk-up flat on the sixth floor with a brilliant roof terrace where we would host numerous parties. Our weekdays saw me working either from HSBC's global headquarters on Queen's Road Central, or travelling to Beijing or Shanghai, where I headed up the offshore business for the bank. At weekends we would stay up into the early hours drinking in the bars of Lan Kwai Fong and Wanchai – or alternatively we'd hop on a plane with our new friends and spend a few days in a Chinese city we had never heard of, or visit the likes of Laos, Cambodia, Bali, Phuket, Borneo and the Philippines.

I quickly passed my Hong Kong banking exams, a pre-requisite before I could officially sell, and began hitting and exceeding the sales targets given to me. Perhaps for the first time in my career, I believed I was seriously well-equipped to do the job in front of me and that there was no one else in my sales team of over forty employees I thought better at selling than myself. As was often the case in Hong Kong at the time, many of my sales were 'closed' in the Mandarin Oriental's famous Captain's Bar, often over a bottle of incredibly expensive wine or a beer swigged from one of their famous pewter tankards.

I was fortunate that China was preparing to host the Olympics and thousands of well-paid international executives from companies such as Nike and Adidas were being relocated to Hong Kong and China and in need of investing some of their excessive salaries.

One thing that immediately struck me about HSBC was the incredibly aggressive sales culture, the likes of which I hadn't witnessed before or since. We were managed by the quantity, not the quality, of our meetings. After every call, email or meeting, we had to mark our activity with a huge black marker pen on a whiteboard in the office and subsequently record it in our Client Relationship Management (CRM) system. Daily, yes daily, our senior management churned out league tables not only for myself and my colleagues in Hong Kong, but for the extended global sales team across seven other countries.

Having a sales team so dispersed around the world provided cultural diversity, which can undoubtedly enhance creativity, local market insights and customer relationships, and we regularly shared best practices collectively as we looked to build a culture of high performance. Such an environment undoubtedly fostered a global mindset and a sense of cross-cultural learning. However, challenges included communication barriers, time zone differences and potential cultural misunderstandings, which occasionally had a negative effect on team cohesion and productivity as we all fought to be noticed within such a competitive environment.

Drink was at the heart of all we did, and I remember one occasion where we hired a Hong Kong tram for a staff fancy-dress evening, myself dressing up as Britney Spears and us all getting home at 7 am before returning to the office an hour later for the start of another day's work. If ever there was an example of a 'work hard, play hard' culture, this was it.

But more than that, HSBC was very much a name-and-shame culture where you either thrived or died – and fortunately for me I was thriving in the environment. I managed to keep my head above the parapet by regularly meeting and exceeding my monthly sales targets, allowing me to avoid any unnecessary attention or criticism from my manager, and even to be rewarded with paid-for trips on occasion.

Others sadly didn't have the same fate. Each month across the global sales teams, a league table ranked how everyone was performing in terms of actual sales rather than pure activity, and if you were in the bottom 10 per cent (effectively the bottom four of the forty-strong global sales team), you would be put on to what was termed a PIP, a Personal Improvement Plan, where you would be micromanaged on an hour-by-hour basis in the hope of increasing your productivity. Remaining in the bottom 10 per cent for three months in a row (not that difficult if you were waiting for a large deal to land or had been on vacation) would lead to automatic dismissal. This was representative of the ruthless environment they encouraged and a level of pressure that many could not stomach. While I for one seemed to thrive in such a setting (I have always had a competitive streak), I did not believe it was the right way to get the best results out of a team – nor the best way to manage clients' money or build relationships. I was concerned that managing by numbers drove the wrong type of activity with staff constantly looking to increase the number of meetings they were attending, rather than increase the quality of meetings they were arranging.

In my mind, such a culture often led to poor investment outcomes for our clients and was directly correlated to the unhealthily high staff turnover that we experienced. Already I was thinking of how I might do things differently if I were to ever launch my own business.

During my time with HSBC, I also witnessed numerous moments where their culture seemed to stifle both innovation and progress – a real surprise to me given all I had read about Asia's recent growth. A word that was regularly muttered by our Hong Kong and Chinese-national colleagues was 'cannot'. We frequently hit a brick wall if we suggested changes to any of the operational processes already in place. On one occasion, I remember allowing a colleague to arrive at the office an hour late one day due to an early-morning dental appointment, something at the time I thought a pretty innocuous and uncontroversial decision. Well, not for HSBC's human resource department. I was hauled in to see a senior director later that morning who proceeded to read out various clauses within my colleague's employment contract that clearly stated working hours were 08.00 to 18.00 with a one-hour break for lunch. It became clear that I had inadvertently helped my colleague commit a serious breach of their employment contract, and I was explicitly warned that there would be consequences if I were to offer such assistance again.

Hong Kong was a hugely vibrant and exciting place to live, and the island existence gave me some of the most wonderful memories and experiences of my life. But all good things must come to an end and three years into our adventure I was offered an opportunity to transition into investment banking, accepting a role with a Dubai-based bank called Shuaa Capital.

Two weeks before we left Hong Kong, I proposed to Claire. The timing was likely influenced by the fact that I was now asking her to move with me to yet another country, and I felt she deserved a true commitment. More importantly, I knew Claire was the most amazing partner in crime and the person I wanted to spend my life with. I proposed with a marshmallow ring on South Bay Beach, knowing I wasn't brave enough to choose a real one without her input. We spent an incredible final two weeks celebrating our engagement and saying goodbye, culminating in a wonderful farewell party at the magnificent Mauritian Embassy, perched on top of Hong Kong's Peak.

Shuaa Capital enticed me to move to the Middle East with a generous package including numerous stock options, the first time I had experienced owning equity in a business for which I worked.

Weekends and holidays were again dominated by travel, and I was lucky enough to visit some fascinating regional countries that I had long dreamt of, such as Syria, Iran, Jordan and Lebanon, experiencing a completely different Middle East to those who might visit Dubai on vacation. We would frequently drive to the Musandam peninsula in Oman, spending weekends on dhow boats where we would swim with dolphins and camp under the stars.

In a well-planned manoeuvre, all three of our children were born in Dubai, prior to the incubation of Health at Hand. We benefited from the great private-health insurance we were afforded through my work and experienced what many called a 'champagne lifestyle on a lemonade income' – living like relative kings and queens with a live-in maid and driver and salary savings sufficient to allow us frequent trips to the UK to attend friends' weddings and family birthdays.

Working for Shuaa Capital was eye-opening. Things were certainly done a little differently in the Middle East, and while risk and compliance teams within international banks were becoming rather prohibitive from a decision-making perspective – and rightly so given the backdrop of the recent financial crisis – the Middle East still seemed like the Wild West. I flew first or business class whenever I travelled with work, and I could stay in pretty much any hotel I wished to on my business trips, often frequenting Raffles Hotel in Singapore and expensing an unlimited number of Singapore Slings (a famous cocktail of pineapple juice, gin, cherry brandy, lime juice, grenadine, triple sec and Benedictine) on my work credit card. I regularly travelled back to Asia, and frequently between the six countries of the Gulf Cooperation Council (a regional political and economic union comprising of Bahrain, Kuwait, Oman, Qatar, Saudi Arabia and the United Arab Emirates), building up a wonderful network of Arab business contacts which I knew would undoubtedly come in handy at a later stage of my career.

Ultimately, Shuaa's over-reliance on offering investments exposed purely to the Middle Eastern markets was perhaps one reason for the steep decline in their share price during my time working for them, meaning my stock options were effectively worthless by the time I left to head up the Bank of Singapore's operations in the Middle East. By now, though, I already had my eye on starting my own business, and I spent far too many hours as a Bank of Singapore employee working on my various business plans.

The story of my career to this point is of huge importance to the story of Health at Hand. While I would encourage others to set up their own businesses a little earlier in their career than I did, and certainly before the financial pressure of having children arrives, I was lucky to be able to draw on so many different experiences as I commenced my journey as an entrepreneur. In my mind, having such a depth of corporate experience before jumping into the deep end was a great benefit, and allowed me to learn from both the good and the bad habits that I had encountered along the way.

So, there we were, the Health at Hand dream team, sitting in a café in the shadow of the world's tallest building, the Burj Khalifa, debating what we wanted the culture of the business to look like. Morgan Stanley's perception was that the longer hours you worked, the better you were at your job and HSBC's perception was that the more meetings you conducted, the greater chance you had of selling. Shuaa Capital were all about bluster and bravado, and at Kleinwort Benson client relationships were valued above all else. I believed none of these approaches to be perfect, but I did know that I wanted to build a culture of carrot over stick – an environment where all staff were supportive of one another, where we collaborated to help each other for the benefit of the business, where we had a flat organisational structure and where people weren't afraid to pose their own ideas and challenge each other. I perceived the aggressive Morgan Stanley and HSBC cultures in particular to be detrimental to both positive client outcomes and to employee satisfaction. I wanted innovation to thrive, but more than anything, I wanted my team to really enjoy their working hours.

Google is one notable example of a company that has successfully utilised a 'carrot over stick' approach. The tech giant is famous for its culture of innovation and employee satisfaction, with a focus on emphasising positive reinforcement and a desire to offer creative workspaces and opportunities for professional growth. This supportive environment has not only allowed them to attract top talent, but has also contributed to them achieving exceptional performance and groundbreaking innovations, proving that investing in employee morale can lead to substantial business success.

I am a strong believer that if you trust your employees, allow them to work how and when they wish and provide them with a supportive and collaborative environment, they will stand by you in times of need or stress, perhaps when you have a crucial contract to get over the line at short notice or when you are firefighting on a particular issue.

My first decision as team leader was an easy one. I wanted to give every single employee ownership in Health at Hand irrespective of their seniority, age or experience. I believe that the culture of collective ownership drives loyalty, decreases staff turnover and builds trust.

I sought my board's approval to create a pool of capital for employees, referred to as an Employee Stock Ownership Plan (ESOP), that would effectively see all investors dilute their shareholding, including myself. I then allocated equity options to current staff and new hires. Equity options are often used above pure equity to drive loyalty. Instead of granting employees full equity upon their start date – risking that they might leave the next day while still holding shares – options are structured to vest only after employees have completed a specified number of months or years with the company. At Health at Hand, equity vested at a rate of 10 per cent after one year of service, 20 per cent after two years, 30 per cent after three years and 40 per cent after four. This vesting schedule provided a significant incentive for staff to remain committed to the company, a particularly important tool that would hopefully allow Health at Hand to retain our talent in the future.

Following our initial investment raise, we rented and renovated a fantastic office space, but I wanted to provide the team with the flexibility to work from home and choose their hours. This was pre-COVID, and remote work was not yet common in many businesses.

This approach was particularly beneficial for team members like Amy, who had a young family; Aftab, who wanted to leave the office early some evenings to explore Dubai's restaurant and cultural scene after moving from Pakistan; and Shiju, our newly hired designer, who was caring for his mother at home.

While client-facing staff, including myself, occasionally needed to wear suits or smart attire for business meetings, I preferred a relaxed dress code in the office and allowed employees to wear whatever they felt comfortable in. Aware of the increasing number of Muslims on our team, I emphasised the importance of respecting cultural and religious differences. To support this, we installed a prayer room on our office floor and established guiding principles regarding the likes of non-Muslims eating in the office during Ramadan, when many team members were fasting.

While we did on occasion arrange nights out to a local bowling alley or cinema, often followed by a meal and alcohol (and Amy and I drank our fair share of red wine together while strategising on how we were to run the business), we ensured these events were voluntary, respecting that we had a team of extroverts, introverts and everything in-between. No one likes organised fun, especially if it's forced on you by the boss.

To respect and understand each other's culture, once a month we arranged a lunchtime picnic in the local park where we would each bring a dish from our home country and share the food amongst our colleagues. This was one of my favourite and best-received ideas, with colleagues socialising while sharing an array of beautifully home cooked dhal, samosas, tahini and cakes. It really was a leveller across such a multi-cultural team, and an incredibly fun and appropriate way to enjoy each other's company. As the CEO, I of course participated in all these activities, and would regularly enjoy making a Victoria Sponge or Eton Mess, with mixed culinary success.

I also introduced the idea of a personal User Guide for each employee, an idea I had cobbled together from reading the stories of various Silicon Valley startups. Essentially, this was a user manual for each member of staff, written by themselves and allowing others to understand them better and empathise with them more. Included in these manuals would be sections on 'how I would like to receive feedback', 'what motivates me' and 'what my colleagues should be aware of'. Our User Guides became a wonderful internal resource, and I found that the most introverted of staff would really open up on paper when they may not have found it easy to do so in person. On reading my colleagues' User Guides I discovered that Nadine was living with her wheelchair-bound grandmother, that Nadia was best avoided before she had drunk her first morning coffee and that Ahmed would ideally like to start work early and finish early each day so that he could support his wife during his children's bath-time each night.

With a few simple and thoughtful initiatives such as those listed above, we quickly became a close-knit team and, more than that, a team with huge respect and empathy for each other. We used Slack to communicate more efficiently as a team, subscribed to Salesforce, a market-leading Client Relationship Management (CRM) system, to track our external communications with clients and prospects, and introduced monthly lunch-and-learn sessions to keep everyone informed about each other's work and the company's strategic direction. Staff were given a learning budget, an extra day off on their birthday and a 'duvet day' where once a year, unannounced, they could take an extra day off without any questions being asked. We went short of offering free meals in the office, but we did introduce free fruit and energy bars, which I would buy from a local supermarket once a week on my way into the office.

It was from this baseline culture that we were able to consult with the staff to build out a more detailed mission, vision and set of values for the business, realising that we had outgrown our original efforts. I believed it important that cultural and strategic decisions now came from the staff as opposed to just myself, and I empowered the team to write their own rules. The staff determined that phones would be banned during lunch breaks, and we committed to 'showing up' and being 'present' throughout the day, which in our world meant being respectful of other people's time and always being on time and participating fully during meetings.

Our large sit-down boardroom table was replaced with a higher, stand-up table, and the chairs were removed, allowing us to introduce what I termed 'micro-meetings'. I am not sure if this idea came from a book I had read, but I never quite understood why business meetings always seemed to last sixty minutes. I had learnt over the years that many decisions didn't take that long, and that most people's concentration spans were much shorter than an hour. And so, at Health at Hand, twenty-minute micro-meetings were born. Of course, on occasion we needed longer meetings or full mornings or afternoons for strategising, but our micro-meetings were designed for maximum efficiency and for us to learn to make decisions quickly.

At times, mid-micro-meeting, we'd realise we needed more than twenty minutes to reach a decision, at which point the person who had originally called the meeting (the 'sponsor') had the authority to extend it by an additional ten minutes at their discretion. However, when that time was up, a decision had to be made. I truly believe that our micro-meeting culture made us more efficient and improved our decision-making.

Building a collaborative and supportive culture does not guarantee success, and I thought long and hard about how I would use this new environment as a springboard to drive what I termed 'high-performance'. To me, moulding our culture was one of the most exciting things about being a business owner. As a founder, no one will ever love the business more than you do, and I was acutely aware of this as I tried to carry the team along with me.

Importantly, while I asked my team to work smarter than the competition, I was adamant that we were never to bad-mouth the competition in public, ever. Instead, we chose to focus on our strengths rather than highlighting the weaknesses of the competition. This approach not only set us apart but also fostered a healthier mindset, allowing us to build on our own capabilities rather than being distracted by our competitors' shortcomings.

I tried to build an environment where we all cared about the problem we were trying to solve, where clinical outcomes were the most important consideration in all decisions we made and where we strove to be market-leaders.

Looking at how corporate culture has evolved in recent years, I believe some of the ideas I introduced to Health at Hand were quite forward-thinking at the time, and I was particularly pleased that we seemed to have a unified team dedicated to the cause, despite the obvious challenges presented by having a multi-cultural staff. Of our first fourteen hires, we had colleagues from seven different countries, including Egypt, Pakistan, India and Syria, covering numerous languages and religions. I was further convinced that our culture was working when I regularly assessed the team's sentiments through staff-satisfaction surveys. These surveys consistently indicated that we were effective in both motivating the team and ensuring a high level of job satisfaction. To me, the truest measure of any culture is what happens when the boss isn't in the room, and I often encouraged my leadership team to share their experiences and observations from times when I was away.

In amongst all this positivity, I was also aware that we were constantly evolving, and I wanted to determine if everyone was the right 'fit' for the business as we grew. It was at this time that I decided we needed a more experienced Chief Medical Officer to fulfil Jenna's role. Jenna was an incredibly positive influence to have around the office. She was great with people and no doubt a very competent doctor, but I sensed that at some point further down the line, our clinical protocols would be greatly tested by a regulatory body and that they would expect us to have someone who had been operating in a Chief Medical Officer role previously.

In the end, Jenna left with most of her equity allocation intact, as I believed she had done an excellent job overall. To support her during her transition, I offered her two months of redundancy pay instead of the one month stipulated in her contract and assisted her in finding a new role. Despite my intentions to be generous, negotiating Jenna's departure was challenging. Her husband James was a lawyer and had previously done pro-bono work for the company, which led to some difficult conversations – some of which I could have handled better. I was delighted when, a few months later, Jenna visited the office, and we embraced warmly before enjoying a lovely lunch with the rest of the team.

As a business owner, you cannot stand still and dwell on challenges for too long. Resilience is a key skill of any entrepreneur, and you need to move on quickly from any hiccups. With the help of

Amy and Aftab, who were quickly becoming my trusted inner sanctum for strategic decisions, we were creating a unified workforce, an environment that allowed innovation to thrive and a culture of high performance. Thoughts of unicorns were certainly on my mind.

KEY TAKEAWAYS

- **Learn from your past experiences.** Consider the good and bad you have experienced in previous jobs and use these insights to build a culture that is both innovative and supportive. Be prepared to do it your way and to tear up the rulebook.
- **Use stock options to incentivise and motivate staff.** Collective ownership drives loyalty and will likely reduce your staff turnover. It also aligns individual success with the company's long-term growth, fostering a deeper sense of purpose.
- **Encourage the use of personal User Manuals to nurture empathetic relationships.** In my experience, this helped Health at Hand's less extroverted staff open up and share, enabling us to build closer bonds. These simple documents created a safe space for honest communication and helped teams understand each other's working styles more deeply.
- **Culture alone is not enough.** Use your culture as a springboard to improve outcomes and drive an environment of high performance. When culture is paired with accountability and clear goals, it becomes a powerful engine for sustained success.

5

WILL IT MAKE THE BOAT GO FASTER?

'Focus is about saying no'

STEVE JOBS, CO-FOUNDER OF APPLE

Even in the relatively early days of Health at Hand, I was continually focused on identifying our potential advantages over our competitors. This next phase of our journey, however, would see us prioritising refinement, optimisation, and strategic planning, positioning us to be market-ready for launch.

To articulate the message of what I called 'ruthless focus', I drew on a phrase that was coined by the British Olympic Rowing Team, one of the most consistently successful teams in world sport over the last forty years: 'Will it make the boat go faster?' The British Olympic Rowing Team had one goal in life – to go faster – and every decision they made was taken through this lens. I loved this simple sentiment and focus. It allowed them to separate the nice-to-haves from the must-haves. Should they spend money on new, high-performance gym equipment? And on a new dietary supplement? And should they hire a new strength and conditioning coach? The answer to all their questions was: only if it made them go faster. Given the simplicity of the messaging, we referred to this key phrase in every product and engineering meeting, and I even had the words printed and stuck on an affirmation wall in our boardroom in two-foot letters so no one would forget!

Cognitive Load Theory was coined in 1988 by John Sweller. In cognitive psychology the load refers to the amount of your working memory that is used. If there is an overload of information, it may lead to personal frustration and a detachment from the details one is attempting to process. As a big believer that human beings can only retain a certain amount of information at any given time and that an overload of information can be hugely detrimental to human performance, it follows that in my thinking this could pose a problem for the performance of a company. In light of this, as the Health at Hand team grew, it was apparent that we came from a variety of different educational and cultural backgrounds. As I have previously alluded to, seven different first languages were spoken within the team – ranging from Urdu and Hindi to English. The diversity of a team can be its super strength – but only if diversity is there for the right reasons and not simply for window-dressing. I didn't want to fall into the trap of hiring more women, more ethnic minorities or more people from the LGBTQ+ community, for example, just for the sake of it or to hit quotas – I wanted a diverse team because I strongly believed that their diverse opinions around the table, drawn from their different life experiences, would be of huge benefit to the business. Being a business located in a cultural hotbed like the UAE, it was nearly inevitable that our team was going to come from a diverse range of backgrounds anyway, but for me this only increased my desire to avoid any unnecessary cognitive overloads and to ensure we were all pointing in the same direction. I was keen that we had a clear and concise roadmap for the business and that everyone connected with the company was on board with the direction of travel. Considering this approach, I wanted to define some simple messaging and goals that the staff could not only recite, but that they could get behind.

We designed our internal learning sessions such that the content broke down complex information into manageable segments, ensuring that each concept was thoroughly understood by the team before moving on to the next. This approach not only improved communication but also increased overall retention of information and engagement. I had witnessed numerous examples across my career of technical product specifications being explained to non-technical staff in a confusing and unhelpful manner and I was keen that we didn't fall into the same trap. I was a good proxy for this idea; given the limitations of my own technological capabilities, if I couldn't grasp what we were trying to achieve, we had to find a simpler way of articulating the message.

I am also a subscriber to Miller's Law, which states that the average person can only keep seven items in their working memory (plus or minus two depending on who you are). This is not to question people's intelligence if they can retain fewer than seven, it's more of a guide as to how the average person processes information. Practically, I wanted to use this knowledge in a way that would benefit Health at Hand, and my first target was for us to define some Key Performance Indicators (KPIs) through the lens of Miller's Law, agreeing on a small number of clear and concise metrics that the whole business could recite and get behind.

A KPI is a quantifiable measure of the performance of a particular objective over time. KPIs are important for a few reasons: they provide targets for businesses and teams to strive towards, they allow you to gauge progress at any moment in time and they help people across the business, particularly those in leadership roles, to make better decisions. Valuing their importance, Amy, Aftab and I sat down each quarter, alongside our newly appointed Chief Medical Officer, Yasmine, to outline our KPIs, our definitions of success and, importantly, how we would measure these. These quarterly planning sessions played a key role in our journey. While there were times when healthy debates arose over our goals, by the end of each session we were all aligned and focused on achieving the same outcomes. This collaborative process helped ensure that everyone was moving forward with a shared vision and a clear direction.

We overlayed the lens of 'SMART' on our KPIs to ensure our work was indeed Specific, Measurable, Achievable, Relevant and Time-bound – and I added one of my own into the mix: were these targets also Stretched, as in stretched to their feasible limit? So, at Health at Hand, we adopted 'Charlie's SMARTS KPIs', a phrase which didn't exactly roll off the tongue, but which ensured we had Specific, Measurable, Achievable, Relevant, Time-bound and Stretched targets. Stretched didn't mean overly ambitious, unattainable goals. It meant always seeking to outperform.

I was also keen that our KPIs weren't a finger in the air guess or a mere wish list of what we *wanted* to achieve. They were a list of what we thought we *could* achieve, albeit if the stars were somewhat aligned.

The next step was to share these KPIs with the wider team and listen to their feedback. As I have previously mentioned, one of the best aspects of starting your own business is the freedom to shape it according to your own vision and values. This autonomy allows entrepreneurs to create a company that truly reflects their goals and principles, making the journey more fulfilling and personal. In my case, I was clear from the outset that I wanted a very flat organisational structure and an environment where people were encouraged to speak up. Hierarchy in a company can be suffocating because it often creates rigid structures where decision-making is centralised, limiting employees' autonomy and creativity. This can lead to a lack of innovation, as lower-level employees may feel hesitant to share ideas or take initiative due to strict chains of command. Additionally, it can foster an environment where communication is inefficient, preventing open collaboration and the free exchange of ideas. When employees are constrained by these factors, it can reduce overall motivation and hinder a company's ability to adapt quickly to changes.

However, slightly amending Winston Churchill's famous phrase, 'Democracy is the worst form of government, except for all the others that have been tried,' I am personally a believer that 'democracy is great, until it's not'. By this I mean that while canvassing the opinion of others is overall a good thing, it can also on occasion slow down the speed and effectiveness of decision-making. So, while I frequently listened to and acted on the opinion of my very capable colleagues, there were occasions where as a leader I believed I had to be bold and take decisions in isolation, by myself.

This is not to say that Health at Hand was a pseudo-democracy – I was very honest about when I wanted help and when I didn't.

Nor was it a 'Potemkin democracy', named after the fake, portable villages built to impress Empress Catherine II of Russia during her visit to Crimea. I liked to think that Health at Hand was an environment where we spoke openly and honestly to each other and where opinions were canvassed fully, when I deemed it necessary.

I was hopeful that these numerous building blocks would complement our desire to create a high-achieving business and add to the high-performance culture I strived for. In respect of Miller's Law, we ultimately came up with five KPIs to start the process, these being:

1) Increase Utilisation: increase the utilisation rates of our app by 5 per cent month on month (utilisation defined as a user who had signed up to the app and used the service at least once).
2) Reduce Waiting Times: decrease the average waiting time to see a doctor via the app by twenty seconds month on month.
3) Reduce Code Churn: reduce the amount of re-written or deleted code by 5 per cent month on month.
4) Improve Clinical Outcomes: increase the number of patients successfully treated by video by 2 per cent month on month (a successful consultation being defined as a video consultation that did not require an additional face-to-face appointment within thirty days).
5) Improve Staff Well-being: achieve an increase in the average score for staff wellness surveys quarter on quarter.

These KPIs were all documented on our shared drive, making them readily accessible at all times to the full team. They were carefully designed so that each mini department or squad within the business had at least 1 KPI to shoot for. Colleagues were required to update their progress in advance of our weekly team catch-up, and the leadership team would then make regular comment on the progress. Regular check-ins were put in everyone's diary to discuss these KPIs, and we arranged quarterly full-company strategy days to determine what changes were required, if any, to these metrics. Such was the focus we put on these guardrails that I am confident many of the Health at Hand team of the time would still be able to recite the majority of these KPIs verbatim.

KPIs are effectively *what* you want to achieve. In my opinion they are ineffective and flawed if considered in isolation. In addition, employees at Health at Hand were required each month to determine *how* they would aim to meet and exceed these indicators by building out specific Standard Operating Procedures (SOPs) for each of the stated goals. My personal interpretation of SOPs was that they were a way of documenting day-to-day processes so as to make actions repeatable. They were heavy on detail and effectively provided a roadmap for staff to follow in their day-to-day activities and proved to be useful when conducting staff one-to-one catchups and appraisals.

Given the fact we were still in our infancy as a business, I had the capacity to straddle all our teams, and I had an input into the KPI setting and the subsequent SOPs across all our teams. Under KPI #1 (Increase Utilisation), for example, the SOPs might detail the steps we would take to make the app onboarding process easier – perhaps by building a simpler sign-up process requiring fewer clicks or by introducing the likes of iris authentication to verify our users' identities. They might also outline how we would aim to improve signposting within the app for easier patient navigation, or how we would go about generating more in-app content to reassure and educate the consumer.

Having established these crucial indicators, we returned to our new guiding mantra, 'Will it make the boat go faster?', making all our decisions based on whether they would indeed help us 'go faster' and allow us to achieve our KPIs. Did we believe that by adding thumbprint app access we would be able to increase the utilisation of the app (KPI #1)? If the answer was yes, we'd prioritise it on our roadmap, and if not, we'd put it in the 'nice to have' category and build the feature only when we had completed our MVP build (see page 43) and had capacity to do so across our engineering team.

It was at this time that we started having issues with our outsourced technology partner, Mokus. Mokus were a technology consultant who were connected to tens if not hundreds of individual freelance engineers across the globe. Their business model was such that they would share the scope of our individual engineering tasks (however big or small) across their global network, and their freelance engineers would pitch to deliver each individual engineering task within a defined timeframe and for a pre-determined cost. This could be a simple task such as 'move this button on our home screen on our Android App from position A to position B', or a more comprehensive task, such as 'build a back-end platform that allows us to onboard third-party doctors with a built-in queuing algorithm and scheduling tool'. Mokus's advantage was that they were low cost, and we could limit the number of people on our direct payroll. Until we were satisfied that the freelancers had 'shipped' their work to us within the negotiated timeframe and to the right standard, we wouldn't need to pay, meaning we reduced the risk of paying for poor quality or incomplete work. Mokus itself merely added a margin to each job for connecting us to their network of developers.

Mokus was led by a Syrian lady called Rima. In the early days of our partnership, Rima and I spent hours and hours in her apartment in Dubai's Motor City, with me brain-dumping everything I wanted to achieve from our product and Rima turning my thoughts into language that an engineer could understand. But there were a couple of big flaws in this model. Firstly, I was not from an engineering background and therefore not skilled enough to scrutinise the responses Rima might give me, such as, 'Oh Charlie, that's a pretty chunky piece of work and is likely to take a senior engineer sixty-five hours to complete.' At this point, Nadim came into his own, with support from Aftab. Having a board member (and friend) from a technology background meant there was a level of integrity around the whole process, and Rima and her team of freelancers were generally kept honest. I strongly encourage all technology entrepreneurs and founders to have someone with an engineering background in a key leadership role at the top of their organisation.

Over time I was becoming increasingly concerned that Mokus's model meant that none of these freelance engineers really understood what the bigger picture of Health at Hand looked like – they were completely disconnected from what we were trying to build and achieve, and they certainly didn't buy into our culture. These third-party engineers merely worked in silos to deliver their individual features and would then send the completed engineering work to Mokus before focusing on another task, either for us or another company.

Our licensing set-up in the DMCC freezone afforded us significant savings when it came to the likes of visas and taxes. We were also able to lean on the support of Astrolabs, a DMCC innovation hub that encouraged the growth of technology businesses in the freezone. During my regular visits to Astrolab's office, I met an incredibly bright and driven Pakistani gentleman called Farzal who ran a successful technology company called Next Generation Innovations (NGI), based out of Karachi, Pakistan.

NGI's model was different to Mokus's in that, while they too helped build technology products for early-stage companies who couldn't necessarily afford to hire their own team on Day One, everyone who worked for NGI was employed directly by them and based either in their Karachi office or on international placements at their clients' offices.

I immediately warmed to Farzal. He was a successful entrepreneur himself, incredibly engaging, and given he spent long periods in Dubai in between his regular trips back to Karachi, we were able to see each other frequently and build a relationship. Farzal was smart. At no cost he came into our office and conducted a comprehensive appraisal of our technology stack and processes, determining which specialist technology engineers and experts he believed we needed to upgrade our technology and where we might be able to drive increased efficiencies and cost savings. He analysed the work Mokus had conducted and offered up more proficient solutions for our future technology build, without ever being directly critical of Mokus's approach.

Farzal himself was also big on team culture, frequently posting on LinkedIn about various milestones his team had achieved. He really cared about those who worked for him, and I soon realised that he shared many of my own values and those of Health at Hand. He was warm, open and generous with his contacts and regularly talked with affection about his colleagues and their families. Most importantly, I trusted him, and after some deliberation, and with the help of Nadim and Aftab, who knew of Farzal through some of his contacts in Pakistan, we made the decision to replace Mokus with NGI. Overnight we effectively had nine full-time engineers based in Karachi, employed by Farzal but all working exclusively for Health at Hand.

I quickly hopped on a plane for the first of my many visits to Pakistan, armed with Health at Hand merchandise including wall banners and laptop stickers to begin the journey of integrating our new Karachi-based team into the Health at Hand culture.

One advantage of our commercial agreement with NGI was its inclusion of an 'aqua-hire' clause, short for acquisition-hire and something that I had not previously been aware of. For early-stage technology companies, the fastest way to build a product is by directly hiring in-house engineers. However, financial constraints often make this impractical. In our case, the aqua-hire model would allow us the use of NGI's outsourced team for now but with the option of acquiring either the full team or individuals on a permanent basis in the future. If successful, key team members could transition to Health at Hand, where we would take on full responsibility for their employment, including visas, health insurance and other benefits. This approach offered flexibility while keeping our business costs manageable.

Farzal and I struck an agreement that, at any stage, if the staff were willing and if Health at Hand could afford it, we could acquire staff permanently from NGI for a fee of one and a half times their annual salary, effectively compensating Farzal for recruiting them in the first place and taking on the risk. I subsequently found out that such a model was viewed incredibly positively by investors. It was proof that we were conscious and careful of our cashflow but forward-thinking enough to have optionality if we wanted to build out our own in-house technology team further down the line. Another advantage of such a structure was that we could, on an ongoing basis, add additional NGI developers to the team, to build-out specific technology features, for a limited period, effectively allowing us to increase and decrease our engineering team size at will and at relatively short notice.

In the years preceding Health at Hand I had been an avid reader of fiction, often having an old classic like *The Catcher in the Rye* or *The Great Gatsby* on the go. Given my drive and determination for Health at Hand to succeed, I no longer had time to read fiction, but instead found myself having two to three business books on my bedside table at any one time. The need to disrupt the healthcare sector had really burrowed deep into my psyche, and many of the books I picked up were along this theme – driving efficiencies, reducing costs, improving access. Embracing the British Rowing Team's mantra, coupled with my own inherent impatience, I was driven to move swiftly toward achieving this goal.

One of the best books I read at this time was *The Patient Will See You Now* by Eric Topol, an American cardiologist, scientist and author whose life mission was seemingly to revolutionise healthcare through individualised medicine. Conceptually the book captured the essence of Health at Hand: a desire to disrupt the primary healthcare landscape and shift the mindset so that patients oversaw their own healthcare rather than it being overseen by their doctors. It was, and still is, staggering to me how little of our personal healthcare history is owned by us, the patients. Often our own doctor's reports are incredibly hard to access, and they are frequently dispersed across a multitude of clinics in the various towns and cities in which we have lived. Reading *The Patient Will See You Now* became a rite of passage for Health at Hand employees and each new joiner was presented with a copy of the book, which I encouraged them to read.

While disrupting the patient-doctor relationship was one thing, in many emerging markets, the main issue for low-income populations was whether they had access to primary healthcare at all, often due to financial constraints.

Access to healthcare was often limited by social class, making it difficult for many to see a doctor. If you were born into a shanty town in South Africa, a favella or a slum in India, your best outcome was often survival. Social mobility was simply not an option, and you were one of the lucky ones if you managed to side-step a terminal disease in your early years. But within a properly functioning developed market, something that the UAE absolutely aspired to be, there was a requirement for a proficient primary, secondary and tertiary healthcare offering for the whole population.

Even in more developed markets, the healthcare sector was and is littered with issues. While the British are extremely proud of their National Health Service, with over 10 percent of Britain's Gross Domestic Product being channelled into the healthcare sector, my opinion at the time was that it really should have been producing much better outcomes than it was. The US healthcare system was also categorised by its high costs, its inequitable access and the unsustainably high price and oversubscription of drugs.

While both preventative care and treatment are critical to a well-rounded healthcare system, there was a noticeable lack of investment in the preventative care side across the Middle East and wider emerging markets. The primary reason for prioritising preventative care is its cost-effectiveness. By promoting regular check-ups, vaccinations, and screenings, health authorities can detect potential health issues early, thereby reducing the need for more costly treatments further down the line. And early intervention saves lives.

Telehealth, as performed by Health at Hand, was very much focused on preventative care over cures. But, while our doctors were perfectly capable of conducting primary healthcare checks on patients via video for issues such as earaches, sore throats, urinary tract infections and common colds, there was obviously a lot that our doctors were unable to do remotely, by video. We needed clear signposting within our apps as to which ailments we were willing to treat, and in which instances patients were best advised to see a doctor physically in a clinic or hospital.

As discussed earlier, we had determined that it was the health insurers who were to pay for our service – after which they would allow their insured patients to access our app free of charge under their insurance plan. While health insurers liked the idea of our service, we still had to convince them of the Return on Investment (ROI), effectively the benefit(s) they would receive by paying for our service. They were unable to write us a cheque unless we proved that Health at Hand could:

a) increase doctor access to their insured populations, or
b) reduce costs

And preferably both.

These were the two primary motivators for the health insurers. They were unwilling to invest into a new technology if it didn't tick one of these boxes and it was only on understanding the health insurer's 'motivation to buy' our product that we believed we had a breakthrough in the problem–solution conundrum that each new business faces.

It is incredibly important to analyse who is paying for your product and why they would want to buy it. A 'nice-to-have' solution is unlikely to be successful. A 'must-have' will give you a chance. Find a solution to a real problem and put yourself in the shoes of the purchaser, considering every conceivable objection they might have to your offering.

Upon conducting a more in-depth analysis of the market and evaluating the results from our initial thousand test consultations, we reached several preliminary conclusions that bolstered our business case. Through the Health at Hand app, we effectively reduced the necessity for patients to make in-person visits for the same issue in 75 percent of cases. The success of our video consultations provided clear evidence that Health at Hand was not only alleviating congestion in waiting rooms but also enhancing patient convenience by enabling individuals to consult with doctors from the comfort of their homes or while on the go.

In addition, the proposed cost of our service to insurance companies was no more than $10 per virtual visit, versus the much higher average cost of a face-to-face doctor visit to the insurer, estimated at between $35 and $55. But more than this, in the face-to-face environment there seemed to be considerable up-selling of prescription drugs, not to mention the manipulation of the system that I had uncovered during my stay in the labour camp. All these factors further increased the incumbent cost of primary healthcare to the insurer. I was aware of no other market model in the world where private sector clinics would achieve commission from a pharmacy for selling their prescription drugs, thereby incentivising them to up-sell the purchase of the likes of opioids where they were not necessarily required.

It got me thinking . . . If Health at Hand could integrate prescription drugs within our app as well, then we would also be able to control the promotion and sale of prescriptions and, in theory, reduce both the unnecessary up-selling of prescription drugs along with the huge and unchallenged costs to the insurers. This approach would no doubt upset the private clinics and pharmacies who were making significant money from these seemingly questionable practices. But hopefully we would delight not just the health insurers but the regulator, whom we had determined were the two most important stakeholders for Health at Hand.

From our analysis, we also concluded that, as we expected, in the Middle East there was a direct and positive correlation between the number of primary healthcare appointments and the reduction in hospitalisations and medical interventions. Primary-healthcare telehealth could in theory reduce the overall burden on the healthcare system, with prescribed early preventative measures like lifestyle modifications significantly reducing the risk or speed at which chronic diseases like diabetes developed.

It is not enough to build a business that sounds good in theory. It must work in practice, and it is fundamental that your idea solves a real problem for whoever is paying for your service. Slowly we were beginning to understand our unique selling points and the solutions we were offering to those who would ultimately pay for our service. We were collecting compelling evidence along the way to back up our arguments, something that we could in turn share with the regulator, the insurance market and potential future investors.

My fierce determination for success saw me aiming high in everything we pursued at Health at Hand. I wanted to ensure that we not only had competitive advantages against any future competition, but that these were sustainable competitive advantages that would stand the test of time. I wasn't afraid to borrow best practices and ideas for those successfully delivering telehealth in other parts of the world. We needed to move fast, and the quicker we built our product and the more partners we onboarded, the higher the barrier to entry would be for the next company trying to enter our sphere.

Aside from having a brilliant technology platform, I also wanted to ensure that the clinical side of our business was the envy of the market. As I have mentioned previously, we had to lead with clinical protocols and patient safety at all times. I was not prepared to compromise on this point, even at the expense of delivering on our KPIs and desired revenue growth.

Given how new telehealth was as a concept in the region, we could potentially become an easy target for naysayers, and without an educated consumer or regulator it was possible that the market simply wouldn't believe that we could treat many primary-healthcare ailments safely via video. We needed to get on the front foot here and become thought-leaders in the space and bastions of good practice. Amy and I worked hard to author and distribute numerous telehealth articles for the regional press as we endeavoured to build my own personal reputation as a thought-leader in the sector. In the subsequent few months, we successfully managed to achieve a number of high-profile speaking slots for myself at events such as the Advance Health Telemedicine Summit in Dubai's Science Park and as a keynote speaker on the Tech Stage at The Future of Digital Healthcare conference in Abu Dhabi. Before too long I was a regular contributor on Dubai's Dubai Eye radio station and I was appointed to the advisory panel for the Dubai Future Council, helping determine the key strategic issues in Dubai, an initiative launched and sponsored by HH Sheikh Hamdan bin Mohammed bin Rashid Al Maktoum, Crown Prince of Dubai and Chairman of the Dubai Executive Council.

Simultaneously, Yasmine was demonstrating her exceptional capabilities as our Chief Medical Officer. As a US Board Certified doctor herself, she embodied a highly esteemed standard, having completed extensive additional training and evaluations beyond her initial medical education and residency. As a team we concluded that going forward, this level of qualification would serve as the minimum standard for onboarding any of our Uber-like suite of third-party doctors. This approach would help us address the concerns of sceptics who may have viewed telehealth as offering a lower standard of care compared to traditional clinics and hospitals.

Initiatives such as this would also set us apart from other rudimentary healthcare solutions available in the market and allow us to answer the questions we frequently received about our clinical quality. Yasmine quite rightly always led with clinical outcomes and patient safety, but she had a rare attribute for a doctor in that she was also innovative and keen to explore my sometimes-preposterous suggestions as to how we might do things differently.

All these steps would allow us to prepare for the inevitable regulatory scrutiny that was to come, and we constantly challenged ourselves to evidence that our video consultations were just as safe as those conducted face-to-face.

Yasmine, with significant input from myself, authored our Doctor Handbook, including outlining our clinical pathways and patient-safety protocols, based on the best-in-class practices we had seen from successful US telehealth companies. We were confident that our work would more than stand the scrutiny of the DHA when the time came to engage with them about achieving a telehealth license.

As a technology-driven business, my vision was for the leadership team to be able to manage Health at Hand from anywhere, even a beach, something only possible if we had reliable and real-time data at our fingertips. We implemented systems to make this a reality. After each consultation, patients were required to rate both the doctor and the platform, as well as provide feedback within the app. To ensure a 100 per cent completion rate for these surveys, we made submitting a rating mandatory before patients could access their doctor's notes in the app, effectively integrating feedback collection into the patient journey. This was a smart technology move, and enabled us to deliver on my remote-management vision.

Our expanding team of doctors was required to write and publish their consultation notes in the app within a maximum of five minutes of each consultation concluding. This efficiency not only delighted our patients but also provided a significant advantage over traditional bricks-and-mortar clinics, where documentation often took much longer to be made available and was invariably owned by the clinic and not the patient. Achieving this five-minute window was feasible for our doctors without compromising quality. And they loved the speed at which this happened nearly as much as our patients did. A common frustration for doctors, both in the region and globally, is the limited time they spend with patients compared to the extensive hours dedicated to administrative tasks like notetaking. One of the key benefits of our app became a major draw for doctors: the opportunity to spend 90 per cent of their day interacting with patients, leaving only 10 per cent for administrative tasks.

The outcome of these patient and doctor-led feedback loops meant that we could rate and analyse each consultation in real time across several different metrics, including the quality of the doctor, what was being treated, the percentage of consultations successfully concluded via video and the satisfaction rating of the patient.

Leaning on some of the maths I had retained from school, we also built a standard-deviation-alert tool into our back-end dashboard. Yasmine and I would be alerted in real time if certain metrics rose or fell significantly above or below their mean, allowing us to intervene in real time. If, for example, our average doctor rating for the month was 4.6 out of 5, we could be notified if any subsequent individual consultation was recorded as being a full standard deviation away from the mean, allowing for our clinical protocols and customer servicing to kick in immediately, where required.

At this stage we had not yet formally launched the business on the open market, and we had a bit of work to do before I was comfortable taking our solution to the DHA for approval. But we were definitely getting there, and we were spending our time learning and refining and learning and refining while collecting a huge amount of data at the same time as our boat began to pick up speed.

All the while, our engineering team were consumed with building our MVP and had little capacity to do anything else. I however wanted to ensure that we didn't get blindsided by all the amazing ideas formulating in our heads, and I worked with the team to devise a roadmap for our product which stack-ranked all the features we required for launch and beyond, prioritising which features we should build first and the time and effort it would take to deliver on each, reminding ourselves to take decisions through the lens of 'will it make the boat go faster?'.

We also added to our team by hiring Taha under our NGI agreement. Taha was an energetic and entrepreneurial engineer also based in Karachi. In quick time we tested the commercial model we had with NGI and relocated Taha permanently from Pakistan to the UAE, the first time he had left his home country. Taha started as our Quality Assurance Manager and was quickly elevated to Quality Assurance Director, such was his positive impact on the business.

One aspect of being a founder that gave me great joy was the positive impact I could potentially have on people's careers, and I loved promoting people on merit if they were doing a good job. Taha had longed to move to Dubai, believing as many did that the streets were paved with gold, and I was delighted that we could make this dream happen for him.

Coming from incredibly humble backgrounds in many cases, our engineering team often saw their titles as more of a motivator than their actual salaries. Status meant everything to them, and I frequently elevated their titles as they proved their worth.

Quality Assurance (QA) refers to the systematic process of ensuring that a company's products or services meet established standards of quality and performance. It focuses on identifying defects and areas of improvement to enhance customer satisfaction and in the context of building a healthcare app, as opposed to a food delivery or ride hailing app, we believed his appointment to be incredibly important.

While much has been written about QA, I firmly believe that it is ineffective when viewed in isolation. QA simply identifies areas of concern without addressing how to implement improvements. To enhance our approach, we expanded Taha's role to include Quality

Improvement (QI), a vital function that enabled us to respond swiftly when we identified quality issues within our product. This strategy allowed us to constantly refine our processes and consistently exceed the high standards we set for ourselves. This emphasis on continuous improvement required a disciplined approach to decision-making, ensuring that every change we made had a positive impact on the business.

By this point we seemed to be working as an incredibly cohesive team, and Farzal's outsourced engineers had both settled in well and were contributing to the culture of the business. Though I was often back and forth to Karachi, I was also conducting numerous early-stage conversations with investors in preparation for our next funding round and constantly networking within the DHA, who were yet to even create a license category for 'telehealth services' – a not insignificant roadblock that I needed to face head-on in the coming weeks.

I was still in regular dialogue with Pat and other global telehealth experts, soaking up as much information as I could. The importance of being a sponge for information was not lost on me, and I am a believer in the 10,000-rule coined by Malcolm Gladwell in his iconic book *Outliers*. Gladwell argued that the key to achieving true expertise in any skill is simply a matter of practising for at least 10,000 hours. I wondered how much better I may have done in my school exams had I had this insatiable appetite to learn a few years before. My simple maths calculation allowed me to conclude that in Gladwell's eyes, I would become a telehealth expert inside two years by working 100-hour weeks.

There are many dilemmas that technology startups and entrepreneurs must consider when deciding the best timing to launch their product into the real world. It's hard to know when you have found a true product-market fit, and it's equally difficult to know when your MVP is ready or when you should share details of your actual product with your potential buyers.

The concept of hypotheses and assumptions revolves around structured decision-making and problem-solving. Hypotheses are testable statements or predictions based on existing knowledge, which can be validated or disproven through experimentation or data analysis. In business, a hypothesis might be: 'Offering free trials will increase patient conversions by 20 per cent.' Assumptions are beliefs or premises taken as being true without immediate proof, often serving as the foundation for hypotheses. For example, an assumption could be: 'Patients will have access to the necessary technology and internet connectivity to participate in telehealth consultations.'

By identifying and testing assumptions through this model, we were able to make informed decisions, allowing us to reduce uncertainty. If we were able to optimise strategies effectively and use this model to test ideas before fully committing resources, we would reduce the risk of costly mistakes. It would also enable us to make data-driven decisions by validating concepts through experiments and real-world feedback. This process was led brilliantly by Amy and through her great skill and hard work we began hosting breakfast workshops with user groups based on our customer profiling.

Many early-stage technology businesses are often reluctant to launch their product until it is 100 per cent market ready, but I am a strong believer that the insights you gain from real users are invaluable and that it's never too early to test your product on the market. Don't get caught in the trap of testing and re-testing your platform in a darkened room with your colleagues, friends and family – the outcomes will be biased, and you will rarely receive honest feedback until you share the product with your real consumers. In my view, the earlier you can test in a live environment, the better. Early market-testing can, in fact, supercharge your growth and your ROI.

While Mark Zuckerberg is not quite as revered today as he once was, he was undoubtedly hugely successful in building Facebook from nothing. Zuckerberg coined a great phrase, 'Move Fast and Break Things', which became Facebook's internal slogan from the day they were founded until around 2014. This approach placed significant emphasis on the speed and adaptability of their team and their ability to ship and share the product with the market quickly.

Zuckerberg urged individuals and teams within Facebook to build solutions fast and without the fear of failure. I recall my Morgan Stanley graduate trainee co-ordinator once saying to me, 'Make lots of mistakes but never the same mistake twice,' and I too wanted to encourage a culture where mistakes were tolerated and where we were bold and brave in our pursuit of excellence. Like Zuckerberg, I was not afraid of us breaking things along the way, and I believed that if our product was perfect at launch, then we'd launched too late.

You won't be surprised to hear that the recently published *Move Fast and Break Things* by Jonathan Taplin (subtitled *How Facebook, Google and Amazon Have Cornered Culture and Undermined Democracy*) became another must-read for the Health at Hand leadership team as we were swept up in the technology explosion surrounding us.

At around this time I also forged a relationship with Ali Parsa, another healthcare entrepreneur, and his wife Marie. Ali had founded Babylon Health a few years earlier. Babylon were the darlings of the European telehealth scene and soon to be the beneficiaries of an investment injection of over $500 million from the Saudi Arabian Sovereign Wealth Fund, the PIF. Babylon's mantra was equally as punchy as that of Facebook: 'Dream Big. Build Fast. Be Brilliant'. Ali was certainly a dreamer and a visionary, with Marie supporting him in a managerial role and for some time on the company's board of directors. I was incredibly impressed by what Babylon were building, and I made a few trips to their office on London's Sloane Avenue where they were happy to show off the Artificial Intelligence (AI) capabilities they were working into a primary-healthcare diagnostics tool for the mass market. They were early movers in the AI space, and I was slightly in awe of what they were building – including their proprietary Digital Twin capabilities, which can build a visual representation of a patient, created using real-time and historical data from wearable devices and electronic health records, and use them to predict and monitor a patient's health status.

Given I was now well known to both the pre-eminent telehealth leader in the US, Dr Pat Basu, and his equivalent in Europe, Ali Parsa, I was in a great position to learn from those a few years ahead of me on their journey. Health at Hand was not seen as a threat to either of these companies, and maybe, just maybe, one of them might be interested in acquiring us in a few years' time.

So here we were – a digital healthcare startup with a dynamic and motivated team, a technology-first cost-containment tool for the health insurance sector and a secure platform enabling patients to achieve effective primary-healthcare outcomes from the comfort of their homes. We were on track to assist the regional government and health regulators of the Middle East in increasing healthcare access while mitigating the corruption associated with the over-prescribing of medication.

Having conducted thorough research and accomplished a great deal in a short period of time, I felt confident that we were ready to formally launch our business. It was time to face our one outstanding obstacle: securing an operating license from the DHA, without which we would be unable to launch.

While the Health at Hand team continued to refine and enhance our product from our offices in Dubai and Karachi, it was my job to secure the required regulatory approvals.

KEY TAKEAWAYS

- **Be single minded in your focus.** As the British Olympic rowing team acknowledged, one rarely has the time and resources to be all things to all people. Analyse what your main goal or goals are and ruthlessly focus on achieving these.
- **Have a clearly articulated strategy.** Chase only a handful of KPIs that everyone in your organisation can repeat and get behind. Confusing messaging is, well, confusing, and the average person can only keep a limited amount of information in their working memory.
- **Go that extra mile and think a little deeper than others.** Key Performance Indicators are no good without Standard Operating Procedures, and Quality Assurance is no good without Quality Improvement. And set yourself stretched targets, not just targets!
- **Move fast and break things.** The best testing you can do is in the 'live' environment – get your product out there and learn quickly. And don't be afraid to make mistakes along the way, but don't make the same mistake twice.

6

READY FOR TAKE-OFF

'The biggest risk is not taking any risk'

MARK ZUCKERBERG, FOUNDER OF FACEBOOK

The Dubai Health Authority (DHA) plays a crucial role in the healthcare system of Dubai, focusing on policymaking, regulation and the delivery of healthcare services. Over the previous few months, myself and my senior team, namely Amy, Aftab and more recently Yasmine, had read page after page of their publications, and where possible, we had attended DHA workshops and roundtables to get closer to their government ministers and leadership teams.

The DHA's mission was to ensure access to high-quality healthcare for residents of Dubai and to promote the overall health and well-being of the community. We agreed with its stated aims, but the nuance of our solution was our particular emphasis on making primary healthcare accessible to *all* and not just the privileged few.

We had been incredibly patient in not sharing our telehealth solution with the DHA too early; we wanted to ensure that Health at Hand was not only fit for purpose before we shared it with one of our most important stakeholders, but that they would be suitably impressed by the professionalism of our offering.

It was also important for us to have an intimate knowledge of the DHA before we attacked. How did they receive their funding? What were their biggest pain points? How did they work with the private sector? What were their strategic priorities?

We had determined that the DHA was funded through a combination of government allocations, healthcare service revenue, insurance premiums, grants and private-sector partnerships. The budgeting process involved strategic planning, proposal submissions, internal reviews, government approval and ongoing monitoring to ensure that resources were used effectively to meet the healthcare needs of Dubai's population.

Their main source of funding came from allocations made by the government of Dubai, essentially the share of public-sector funding allocated to healthcare infrastructure, services and public health initiatives, and we were buoyed by the increasingly large budget being allocated to primary healthcare, technology solutions and preventative care over the preceding few years.

Aside from being the chief regulator of everything healthcare-related, setting the standards and regulations for healthcare providers, and ensuring that healthcare facilities, professionals and services met stringent quality and safety standards, the DHA also operated their own revenue-generating hospitals, clinics and medical centres. They charged for outpatient visits, inpatient care, surgeries and other medical procedures and received payments from health-insurance providers for covered serviced rendered to patients.

They would on occasion receive grants and donations from international organisations and private donors, and they were seemingly open to collaborating with the private sector where they lacked the expertise, investment or resources.

I had already met a handful of the DHA's executive team in informal settings, and they all knew a formal meeting was imminent. I had been a little guarded about what we were building at Health at Hand. I was aware that they were exploring the use of telehealth to drive efficiencies in the healthcare system and that this was high on their agenda. But I also knew that they didn't have the in-house expertise or intention to build their own solution.

I was particularly encouraged by the DHA's focus on preventative care, being strong believers, as we were, that focusing on prevention was money well spent, particularly in a market where chronic diseases such as diabetes and obesity were as prevalent as anywhere in the world.

While technology and innovation seldom featured in their documentation, and they gave very few specific examples of what any technology-led solution might look like, they did explicitly comment within their marketing documentation that 'it was part of their mission to promote the adoption of innovative technologies and practices in healthcare, aiming to enhance the efficiency and effectiveness of healthcare delivery'.

As the health regulator, we absolutely needed the DHA onside. At this point there wasn't even any legislation allowing a telehealth or digital-healthcare company to operate in Dubai. I wondered how long it might take to convince the DHA that regulating telehealth activities was a good idea. We had to present a brilliantly well-researched solution that was solving a real problem, and we needed to point to other international markets where telehealth had not only been successfully introduced, but where healthcare outcomes were improving as a result.

Pat was incredibly useful at this juncture. I reconnected with him and delved into what he had presented to the state regulator in San Francisco on launching Doctor on Demand and understood which data points he found helpful when in discussion with the San Francisco Health Commission. We needed to proactively anticipate all the questions that the DHA might throw at us. Meticulous preparation was an absolute necessity.

The DHA's main building was located in the Al Jaddaf area of Dubai, easily accessible to us – just a minute's walk from its closest metro station and a thirty-minute journey from the Health at Hand office on the city's relatively new driverless train. Over the next four years I would make the journey with regularity.

As with many of the Dubai government departments I had previously dealt with, be it the Dubai Roads and Transport Authority or the Dubai Visa Authority, English was not spoken widely amongst the staff and on arrival at government buildings, it was incredibly difficult to determine which floor you should be on, let alone which specific queue you needed to join. My frustration would often boil over at the lack of signposting and efficiency, with hours and hours wasted in queuing for the most mundane of documents.

Given the importance of a telehealth license to the future of Health at Hand, I showed uncharacteristic patience as I navigated through the various departments within the DHA building to reach the Regulation and Licensing Department, right next to the private office of the Minister of Health. When my number was finally called, I was ushered to one of the many administrative clerks sat in a cramped booth and asked how they might be able to help me.

'I'd love to speak to the person responsible for writing healthcare regulation, please?' I said to a rather surprised Emirati lady. 'I am the owner of a private-sector technology business, which I believe can transform the delivery of primary healthcare in the region.' Blank looks followed and my words fell on deaf ears. Mine was a rather unconventional request. It seemed likely that I would have to play the long game and after being further introduced to two or three other clerks, I was moved between several more rooms where I continued to receive confused glances.

Perhaps entering the DHA office and queuing for an appointment wasn't the best approach. I questioned whether I should have cultivated deeper relationships within the DHA prior to this meeting. Perhaps by now I should have had a senior minister on side who could champion my cause within the DHA.

I ultimately left the DHA office empty-handed and realised that I needed to revise my approach. I decided to write to a few of my senior healthcare connections, be they the CEOs of some of the large regional health insurance companies or the managing directors of a number or regional hospitals, all of whom I'd networked extensively with in the preceding few months. Determined as ever, I was asking for an introduction to the most senior contact I could achieve at the DHA in the hope that both my own personal connections and the Health at Hand business model were sufficiently persuasive to open doors.

It was at the same time, with Amy's great help, that the name of Health at Hand was getting out into the market. I had by now authored five or six blogs and articles, shared via our own website and on LinkedIn. I had spoken at a number of technology, innovation and health-tech summits and conferences, either in Dubai or while travelling to another of the surrounding Gulf Cooperation Council countries.

Much was being written at the time on the emergence of Saudi Arabia as a regional super-power. Thus far, the economy of Saudi Arabia was dominated by their considerable oil and gas reserves. Proven oil reserves were estimated to be around 266 billion barrels, making them one of the top two largest oil-producing countries in the world, along with Venezuela. Their gas reserves were also not to be sniffed at either, approximately 300 trillion cubic feet of it, also putting them in the top ten gas-producing countries globally. Recently, and not before time, there was a movement from the government of Saudi Arabia to reinvest their gross domestic profit into non-oil and gas sectors, with their education and healthcare sectors both being major beneficiaries of this capital inflow.

Having a considerably larger population than that of the other five GCC countries combined (around 32.5 million people compared to the UAE – the second most populated country in the region – at approximately 9.25 million), there was no doubt that all regional eyes were on the Kingdom.

I particularly remember travelling to Saudi Arabia's capital, Riyadh, to participate in a panel discussion at their flagship annual healthcare event, the Saudi Healthcare Privatization Conference. On landing at Riyadh International Airport, I received a panicked call from the conference organiser pleading with me to not only host my designated panel, but chair the whole conference, including the delivery of a thirty-minute keynote speech to open the event!

I certainly wasn't one to turn down such an opportunity, but the irony wasn't lost on me. Me, chairing a regional healthcare conference in Saudi Arabia, having only started to study the sector a few months earlier. The Middle East really was a land of opportunity, a place where you could reinvent yourself and become a respected thought-leader in no time. Amy and I were particularly encouraged by the publicity we might receive from my speedy elevation to healthcare guru, but at the same time we reminded ourselves that the population of the region was only a fraction of that in the US, Europe, Asia or Africa. It was no bad thing that I was becoming a relatively big fish, but it was in a small pond.

By the time I arrived in Riyadh, it had become clear that Health at Hand had first-mover advantage in the region. At the time, no one else was really operating in the digital healthcare space – but the region certainly had an interest in what we were building. This was a wave we wanted to ride, and in the absence of a prepared keynote speech, I gave an abridged version of the Health at Hand business plan to the conference delegates, effectively marketing the business to a room of over 600 senior healthcare experts.

By now I had managed to achieve a direct introduction to Abdul Al Mazrouei, a senior executive at the Dubai Health Authority, from an introduction from the CEO of Oman's largest health-insurance company, Dhofar Insurance Company.

I kicked myself that I hadn't taken this route sooner, but as the phrase goes, 'make lots of mistakes but only the same mistake once'. I had acted quickly on making a false step and found an alternative solution quickly. A key lesson here was that a warm introduction to someone senior was obviously much better than approaching the task cold, and certainly better than me simply walking into the DHA offices and hoping for the best.

I began to research Abdul Rahman in as much detail as I could before our upcoming meeting. What was his background? What had motivated him to get to where he had? How could Health at Hand help him meet his own personal KPIs? Had he previously spoken publicly about the benefits of technology and innovation in healthcare? Did we share a love of sport or travel?

My research highlighted that Abdul had long been regarded as a prominent figure in the UAE healthcare sector. He was known for his leadership, his vision and his commitment to advancing healthcare services and public-health initiatives. He had already achieved much in his role and had contributed greatly to the well-being of the UAE's residents, championing their cause.

He was also part of a team that was directly responsible for mandating for the first time in Dubai's history that health insurance *had* to be offered to everyone living and working in Dubai, a significant step in improving the quality of life for the population. Unlike other government departments, the DHA had a reputation for being open, collaborative and willing to modernise, and I was confident that we would at the very least have a positive initial conversation.

It had never been more important to be prepared for a meeting, even more so than my one with Dr Pat all those months ago in San Francisco. Abdul Rahman had the power to shut down Health at Hand before we'd even started, and while I knew we would likely get licensed in Saudi Arabia, I believed that the UAE, and Dubai specifically, was a great place to commence our journey.

I also knew that the DHA had their own cost-reduction targets, which were pretty ambitions and impossible to achieve without the use of technology. It would be a significant challenge for them to deliver on their desire for all residents to have access to health insurance without the introduction of telehealth. I was aware too that they had other goals to improve the overall health of the population, with obesity becoming an increasingly expensive societal issue amongst the young population of Emirati nationals, and that we could potentially help them achieve these.

As always, I tried not to hide behind my pre-prepared presentation, and on arriving in his office I spent time listening to Abdul (as he asked me to call him) articulate the challenges he faced, all of which I knew from my research, while I in turn contributed the specific features of Health at Hand that I believed could help to solve them. I had pre-prepared answers to address his concerns about the clinical quality and outcomes associated with remote primary healthcare, and I persuaded him of the benefits of reducing the reliance of in-person visits, playing on the strain that in-person visits were having on the general healthcare infrastructure and the corruption associated with the over-prescribing of drugs.

Abdul listened intently. He seemingly loved the fact we were a Dubai homegrown startup looking to pioneer a solution that had worked successfully in other larger markets such as the US and the UK. In short, as meetings go, it was near perfect, and we concluded that I would help him and his team draft the Dubai telehealth regulation, which would hopefully mean that he would fast-track the regulation into law to ensure Health at Hand could launch within three to four months.

This was another pinch-yourself moment in our journey. I had the incredible responsibility of helping draft the telehealth regulation for the DHA.

Suffice to say, my first draft hit Abdul's desk some forty-eight hours later, after a couple of late nights cobbling together the best of the US and the UK regulations, and the dream of Health at Hand was starting to feel a little more like a reality.

*

Away from the DHA, and aside from the work we had been doing on building out our technology platform (led by Aftab), marketing and promoting our service (Amy) and ensuring we had robust clinical protocols in place (Yasmine), we now needed to secure enough doctors on the platform to achieve our ambitious patient waiting times to see a doctor.

As a business, we were pre-launch, making no money and spending about $100,000 a month. I determined that the best route to hiring doctors was to employ an Uber-like model, as we did not have the financial firepower to employ tens of our own doctors. But the problem was, as mentioned earlier, that a doctor's licence to operate was essentially owned by the clinic or hospital that employed them. Fortunately, however, we discovered a loophole in doctor licensing that allowed Health at Hand to engage doctors outside their regular working hours, provided their clinics granted permission. The Health at Hand advantage for doctors was that they were able to work from the comfort of their own home with no commute time or cost to get to work, and no risk of picking up any unsavoury illnesses from their patients. They would have significantly fewer administrative tasks to perform for Health at Hand versus the face-to-face environment, and doctors with a young family in particular would likely find that the flexibility offered by Health at Hand really worked around their lifestyle.

Yasmine was on board with this model but also keen that we additionally hire two or three full-time, in-house doctors of our own to help with other work, such as interviewing and onboarding new doctors, updating our clinical protocols and doctor handbook on an ongoing basis, and working with our engineers to enhance our queueing algorithms so that we had sufficient doctors on the platform during busier times of the day.

Dr Becky, an experienced British physician, became our first full-time in-house doctor. She demonstrated remarkable patience during her initial months as our consultation volumes gradually increased from a modest base. Committing to work twenty hours a week from our office and an additional twenty hours from home allowed her to care for her young daughter after nursery each day.

Becky appreciated that Health at Hand allowed her to still perform clinical work from the comfort of her own home while also enjoying the modern, non-clinical environment of our office. The fun and inclusive atmosphere we fostered was a refreshing change from her previous experiences. Our flexible work model enabled her to spend more quality time with her daughter while maintaining a stable income. This balance was a testament to our commitment to supporting a healthy work-life dynamic, proving that a successful career and a fulfilling family life could go hand in hand.

Becky was soon joined by two other full-time Health at Hand doctors, and while Yasmine spent most of her time in her capacity as Chief Medical Officer, she was also available to consult with patients when demand required.

Things were beginning to fall into place for Health at Hand, and Abdul at the DHA was true to his word in fast-tracking telehealth as a regulated activity. We had a minor celebration when we finally saw the telehealth licensing code appear on the DHA website.

Having completed the associated documentation required to guarantee our telehealth license, the final step was an inspection of our premises by the DHA's licensing team. We naively thought that this would be a quick and unchallenging process, and that the junior 'Licensing Official', named Fahd, would pose us few problems. But as I had often found the case in the region, much was lost in translation and misunderstanding. On successfully sailing through the majority of Fahd's tick-box list of questions, he then asked us to confirm that we had a stethoscope on the premises. Offering a *virtual* doctor service as we did, we obviously had no intention of ever seeing patients in our office, and while we understood the necessity of proving we had a fire-extinguisher in the office and that staff had access to a fire exit, a telehealth company offering a remote service should not have been required to have any medical equipment on site, including a stethoscope.

It seemed that the telehealth documents in Fahd's possession contained the requirements that were needed for physical clinics to achieve their license, rather than virtual clinics. It certainly wasn't Fahd's fault, he was merely the messenger, but sadly it meant that we failed our initial office inspection and we would have to wait longer for the green light to launch.

The frustration of another three-week wait did, however, allow us time to fine tune our offering, and it ultimately meant that our DHA license was granted on the same day that the App Store and Google Play approved our iOS and Android apps.

Any technology entrepreneur will tell you of the joy and excitement they feel when their app is finally available on the App Store and Google Play, and we were no different. This was a momentous day for Health at Hand and Amy, Aftab and I celebrated with dinner on the beach. It was finally time to put our launch strategy into action, in preparation for going live.

Now that we had the green light from the government, we were able to supplement the in-house clinical team of three in preparation for the day we launched. We signed agreements with three third-party clinics in Dubai, all of whom were willing to allow their doctors to operate on the Health at Hand platform when they were not seeing patients in-clinic. We specifically targeted clinic groups where we believed the doctors a) met our clinical standards and b) we knew that they had an over-supply of doctors, something termed 'empty-wait-time'. Empty-wait-time is a problem regularly experienced by the likes of delivery companies, whose biggest challenge is to ensure they have sufficient drivers on their platform to maintain short delivery times during peak hours without paying excessive salaries to drivers with little to do during off-peak times. Drivers, and in our case doctors, were likely to be less motivated to work for the platform if they were to receive a lower fee while waiting for work and if there were consistently long waiting times between seeing customers. From a technology perspective, we needed to ensure that we optimised our routing algorithms in order to balance supply and demand efficiently.

Yasmine looked to continually improve our customer service levels and regularly drew up additional clinical and non-clinical protocols, including some consistent language that our doctors would all use at the start and end of each consultation, and the requirement for them to display the Health at Hand logo in the background during their video calls.

We were keen to ensure the experience was the same irrespective of the doctor a patient happened to be paired with, and that our DNA ran through the entire healthcare delivery process. In total, at our peak, we had 192 third party doctors trained to operate on the Health at Hand platform all operating on a brilliant doctor-scheduling tool built by our engineers, not dissimilar to the one used by Uber.

On commencing their shifts, our doctors would be fed a number of analytics through their doctor dashboard. They were able to see the average number of patients and wait times we had experienced that day and study predictive data that would estimate when we would experience peak times, allowing them in turn to determine their potential earnings for an upcoming shift. We made the doctor web-portal as easy to use and informative as we could, including an encyclopaedia of medical terms, links to local pharmacies and our clinical protocols, easy-to-access guides to common ailments, as well as providing training videos surrounding the use of our technology, how to submit their doctor notes and what to do in the event of an emergency.

Given all our doctors had to prove they were trained up to US Board Certification or the equivalent and we were only dealing with primary, non-emergency healthcare, all the Health at Hand doctors were able to consult with all our patients. This really helped simplify our queuing algorithms as we had no need to match a child with a specialist paediatric doctor, for example.

While 'sat' in our virtual waiting room within the app, patients would type in details of their presenting symptoms, which could be viewed by our doctors in advance of starting the call. Patients were then able to see their doctor's medical certification, photograph and biography, all adding to the trust that we hoped to foster in our service.

Data protection is crucial for any telehealth business, as patients entrust us with their most sensitive personal and medical information. Recognising this responsibility, we were committed to not only meeting but exceeding international data protection standards. This dedication was central to building and maintaining trust with our patients, ensuring they felt secure using our platform. By prioritising rigorous security measures and transparent data practices, we aimed to provide a service that was both reliable and respectful of patient privacy and in our monthly strategy meetings we constantly reminded ourselves that we were running a healthcare business and not a food delivery app, which meant crucial decisions were always made with our patients in mind.

In early testing, our waiting times to see a doctor had been just over two minutes, and the average consultation length was fourteen minutes. We really had a chance to make a hugely positive impact on the market. Prior to the launch of our service, if you had a child with a nasty earache in the middle of the night you would have had to drive to a clinic and wait in line until a doctor was available to see you. For non-emergency issues, including drive time, we believed the average time to see a doctor was about three hours. Our huge advantage was that, via Health at Hand, a patient could consult with a US Board Certified doctor within a matter of minutes, day or night, from anywhere in the world.

As I reflected on our doctor model, though, it quickly became clear that we needed to pay our Dubai-based doctors more for night shifts than for day shifts – an obvious oversight in my initial financial projections.

The disparity between day and night shift costs posed a potential long-term issue for Health at Hand's margins. My goal was to democratise primary healthcare by ensuring that our fees remained consistent, regardless of whether patients sought help during the day or at night, so we needed a quick and effective remedy.

As a team, we concluded that the answer lay in onboarding doctors from different time zones. Unlike Uber drivers, our telehealth model didn't require our doctors to be physically near their patients. Within weeks, we partnered with a clinic chain in the Australian outback and onboarded forty-five of their doctors. These doctors met our minimum qualification standards, had ample availability due to low patient volumes in Australia, and, most importantly, were happy to be paid a day rate for covering night shifts in Dubai, thanks to the time-zone difference.

When faced with challenges like these, our high-performance culture meant we tackled issues head-on with urgency and determination, never losing momentum. This resilience, paired with our drive for quick and innovative solutions, allowed us to resolve problems efficiently and keep moving forward.

The formal launch of Health at Hand was an exciting milestone in our brief history, even if the actual number of consultations took a little time to grow into a meaningful amount that we could be proud of.

After months of relentless hard work, countless late nights, and unwavering dedication, finally launching our telehealth business felt like a monumental achievement. It was a moment of pure relief, knowing that all our efforts had culminated in bringing our vision to life. This was no solo journey: it was the result of a true team game, where every member of the Health at Hand team had contributed their skills, passion, and resilience. We felt a deep sense of gratitude for the trust and support we had in each other, which kept us pushing forward even on the toughest days. As we watched our platform go live, elation and excitement filled the room, sparking a renewed sense of purpose for the journey that lay ahead.

Amy had devised a multi-pronged launch strategy based on our four pillars of Awareness, Education, Trust and Utilization.

Awareness of our application was obviously a crucial step. The challenge with a healthcare app is that it is not something that consumers necessarily use daily, unlike a ride-hailing app or food-delivery app. How could we therefore not only let the market know we existed, but ensure that consumers still remembered us – and their password – in times of need? Fortunately, we had anticipated this challenge, and we launched the app with thumbprint access, so that patients or caregivers were not stumbling around for their password as they looked to connect with a doctor in a moment of heightened stress.

We had done much work on how consumers decide which applications appear on the home screen of their mobile devices and how frequently people do their app 'housekeeping', essentially the process of deleting applications that they had not used for some time.

The workshops we had previously hosted with our target consumers proved to be invaluable, be they expatriate mothers who were responsible for the health needs of their household (the so called 'Jumeirah Janes'), or young male professionals becoming more and more reliant on the growing on-demand economy (the 'Fast Faisals'). We continually referenced these user types in our weekly discussion and internally we re-named the on-demand economy in the Middle East the 'Yalla Economy', *yalla* being a Middle Eastern slang term for 'let's go' or 'hurry up'.

Education and the fostering of trust were fundamental to people not only downloading the Health at Hand app, but to them actually understanding what this new telehealth phenomenon was all about and believing that it could provide results that were at least as good as seeing a doctor face-to-face. Even more so than other apps and sectors we had studied, we believed these two pillars to be of fundamental importance to the success of our telehealth business. We built a number of educational tools within the app to help reassure our consumers, and we continually added to the patient endorsement quotes and videos on our website.

And as far as the final pillar of utilisation was concerned, I had learnt from my banking days that winning *new customers* was the hardest type of acquisition but persuading customers to return for subsequent visits, *client retention*, was in theory much easier, particularly if the consumer's initial experience and outcome was a positive one. We knew that we had to delight our patients on their first visit through offering a great and intuitive service at a low cost.

When we first went live, our customer base consisted entirely of direct business-to-consumer (B2C) users. Individuals paid out of their own pocket to access our service, either on a pay-as-you-go basis or through a quarterly or annual subscription for unlimited usage. The pricing strategy we introduced was shaped by:

a) our cost base, the most significant cost being that of the doctor, and
b) our desire to undercut the cost of visiting a clinic in person.

Importantly, now we were live, we were able to track all the metrics we had previously spoken about. Each consultation threw out some invaluable data, including patient and doctor satisfaction ratings, uptime of the technology, average waiting time and the empty-wait-time of doctors. As we had predicted, we were thrown scenarios we had not anticipated on a nearly daily basis, completely in line with my thinking that you never truly know what to expect until you launch an application into the real world. Overall, though, we had been incredibly thorough in our planning.

Reassuringly, the clinical quality of our consultations was extremely high. We had obviously signposted well within the app that our service was for primary, non-emergency issues only, and, besides, we had a robust triage system in place if we found patients were visiting us with healthcare issues that we could not solve remotely. Our early data showed that well over 70 per cent of our consultations were being successfully concluded over video, a data-point that we would begin to use in our marketing outreach. We were hugely reassured that patients and doctors were enjoying using our service and that local online and print media outlets were excited to report about this new and innovative business that was a welcome addition to the technology ecosystem of the UAE.

As our consultation numbers grew, so did our confidence, which encouraged me when speaking to potential insurance partners. Remembering the advice a banking colleague of mine had once told me, 'Fake it till you make it', externally we hinted at a level of interest in our service that we possibly aspired to achieve, rather than one that we were achieving at the time. I was keen, however, that we would never tell any mistruths, and I continued to impress upon the team not to speak in derogatory terms about anyone else in the market. 'Kill them with kindness' was our mantra!

Amy and I were in the same social circle and counted amongst our friends Georgia Tolley, who presented the flagship business programme on the local radio station. Daily, Georgia would interview captains of industry on her show, and in the weeks after our launch she kindly offered to interview me on the radio a few times.

Being a friend, Georgia asked me several gentle, pre-disclosed questions that really played to Health at Hand's strengths. I loved these interviews and rather than using them as a gratuitous marketing exercise, I focused on our mission, vision and values, relating the conversation back to our desire to make primary healthcare accessible to all, our desire to achieve successful clinical outcomes and our dream of mobilising the city of Dubai by offering a trusted, on-demand service that people could use whenever and wherever they needed it.

While I cannot accurately say that we were the talk of the town, there was a moment when we really felt the weight of the city was behind us. I was nominated for several technology and entrepreneurial awards which culminated in me winning the Telehealth CEO of the Year for Europe, Middle East and Africa, and I appeared on the front cover of *CEO Monthly* magazine.

At the same time, I and five other technology entrepreneurs were asked to sit on a government Innovation Committee, hand-selected by the private office of H.E. Sheikh Mohammed, Prime Minister of the United Arab Emirates and Ruler of Dubai. This was a great coup and further elevated my status in the community as a trusted thought-leader in the technology space.

I was aware that we were on the crest of a wave, and while I knew that these times were unlikely to last forever, I was determined that we keep up the momentum. Emotionally my sense of relief at having launched the business had passed, and I was focused on insuring that we were able to fully execute on this opportunity.

KEY TAKEAWAYS

- **Fall in love with the problem, not the solution.** In my early interactions with the DHA, I had a very clear focus on their problem and then adapted our solution accordingly. Don't just hide behind your corporate presentation and expect it to solve everything. Take time to listen, pause and then adapt your business model.
- **A warm introduction to someone is always the best way of gaining their attention.** I learnt the hard way by initially walking into the DHA building and believing I could navigate my way to the right department on my own. How wrong I was.
- **Embrace innovative thinking.** At Health at Hand, we wanted to avoid imposing higher fees for out-of-hours consultations. We quickly devised a creative solution by replacing Dubai-based doctors on night shift rates with Australian-based doctors on day rates, taking advantage of their favourable time difference.
- **Take the good publicity and run with it.** There was a moment where Health at Hand and I were receiving seemingly endless positive press coverage. When things are going your way, push, and then push harder.

7

GET YOUR SPACE BOOTS ON, THIS ONE'S GOING TO THE MOON

'Let others lead small lives, but not you'

JIM ROHN, ENTREPRENEUR AND SPEAKER

In the mid 2000's, Danish brewing company Carlsberg ran a series of brilliant television advertisements as part of a hugely successful marketing campaign. The campaign used the slogan 'If Carlsberg Did', followed by a scenario that showcased an ideal or exaggerated version of a product or service, humorously implying that if Carlsberg were to create these things, they would be the best in the world.

The campaign was devised by London advertising agency FOLD7 and won numerous awards. The phrase 'If Carlsberg Did' became one of the most widely identifiable advertising tag lines of the last fifty years. It loudly proclaimed that Carlsberg were the best at what they did, without referencing their inferior competition or upsetting the advertising watchdogs.

My favourite iteration of this campaign was the television advert 'If Carlsberg Did Nightclubs', which depicted a utopian nightclub experience including no queues or dress-code, an unlimited supply of taxis outside and, of course, free beer.

Due to its flexible and relatable concept, the 'If Carlsberg Did' campaign had a long lifespan, with new ads being released over several years. The campaign significantly strengthened Carlsberg's image as a premium beer brand, with a sense of humour and creativity, and generated positive engagement and word-of-mouth promotion.

For whatever reason, these advertisements had remained in my mind, and on building Health at Hand I was keen that we aimed high in every aspect of the business. 'If Carlsberg Did Telehealth', I wondered which features they would include in the television advertisement to indicate that they were the best of the best?

We knew at the time that Health at Hand had some distinct competitive advantages, and while we had no direct competition offering a similar service in the Middle East, we were aware that it was only a matter of time before a competitor arrived. I often talked to the team about our so-called 'first mover advantage' actually being a 'first mover disadvantage' to ensure that we didn't become complacent. We were launching a brand-new concept and trying to change a consumer-behaviour habit that had been in place for centuries, seeing a doctor in person. Telehealth was nothing like having your pizza delivered to your door versus going to collect it from your local restaurant. We had to convince the consumer that our service was clinically brilliant on top of being convenient.

In these early months we determined that our competition was in fact a patient's local doctor clinic – in other words, the status quo.

Consumers had a choice:

a) to continue consuming healthcare as they always had by visiting a clinic face-to-face at their point of need, or
b) to trust a new way of receiving their healthcare via Health at Hand.

I have always found it useful for companies to revisit their competitive advantages every six months or so, and at Health at Hand we regularly conducted this exercise as a full team in order to canvass a diverse set of opinions and to ensure that we didn't miss anything.

Suffice to say, at launch we had a number of distinct advantages over our competition, which we constantly used in our marketing material and messaging:

1) Lower cost: we offered a significantly cheaper primary-healthcare product when compared to visiting a doctor face-to-face. We would regularly check our price point so we could quantify this cost saving.
2) Shorter wait times: our current wait times to see a doctor were tracking at just over two minutes, which for a panicked mother in the middle of the night or a worried elderly patient presented a huge advantage over the alternative.
3) Convenience: a telehealth consultation with Health at Hand could in theory be conducted from anywhere in the world, providing flexibility and convenience for patients. We were able to track patients accessing the app from oil rigs, desert camps and from the beach in the Maldives to prove out our use-cases.

4) Clinical quality: the clinical quality of our consultations was higher than most had predicted and even higher than the numbers we had seen coming out of the US. But this was a tricky one to shout about – while the clinical quality of our consultations was high, could we ever claim it to be of a higher quality than those in a face-to-face environment? We could perhaps claim that given all our doctors were US Board Certified as a minimum, we had higher doctor's standards than many of the physical clinics in the Middle East, but to confidently claim the clinical quality was higher was a tough one.
5) Doctor notes: one of the many overlooked advantages of telehealth, particularly in the way *we* were delivering the service, was that a patient's doctor notes were shared with them within five minutes of a consultation and would thereafter be available for patients to upload, download and share at any time. This was unprecedented in the face-to-face environment, and we had heard numerous tales of patients having their doctor notes spread across multiple clinics in multiple countries – without being able to assess them themselves.

Analysing your own competitive advantages inevitably comes with a certain amount of personal bias, but as a team we always tried to be as honest as we could in our appraisal of our business. Amy was great at this, often probing and questioning where others may not have done so. Our longstanding personal friendship gave her the confidence to speak up where others may have been more reserved, and she was proof that working with friends was not always a bad idea.

It wasn't enough to simply analyse our competitive advantages. We needed to dig deeper and determine which features of the business were 'nice-to-have' and which were actually game-changers for our stakeholders. To do this we grappled with the questions at the core of the business. Was the convenience of our service sufficient to persuade consumers to use Health at Hand in a time of need? Did people really care enough about having their doctor notes within an app to change how they consumed healthcare? Would our consumers be sufficiently convinced that diagnosing over video really was as safe as in the face-to-face environment?

We determined that competitive advantages #1, #2 and #3 above really were significant and compelling for Health at Hand, and more than that, we believed that they appealed to the health insurance companies we were trying to partner with in addition to direct consumers.

Furthermore, we wanted to maintain a sustainable competitive advantage over time. Much like the team at FOLD7 did with their Carlsberg adverts, I began to explore what other features we could offer within our application to really delight our stakeholders.

As our consultation numbers grew, I had a nagging issue with our offering, something which others on the team were not as worried about but that I really wanted to solve. If during a Health at Hand doctor consultation one of our patients was prescribed drugs or told to purchase over-the-counter medicine from their local pharmacy, they would still have to go to physically buy the item(s). In my mind, it slightly diluted our offering of 'convenience' if a patient might indeed have to get into their car, pay for parking and wait in a queue, wasting a portion of their day – something that we were trying to alleviate via our remote service.

The solution we came up with was to integrate drug and pharmacy delivery within our app. This really was a pioneering offering, even when compared with many of the telehealth companies that were performing well in more developed markets, and would allow us to close the loop by offering a full A–Z service.

The reality was that the technology we would have to build to offer this additional service was just a refinement of the technology that allowed restaurants to deliver to your door, but I believed it would be a game-changer for our business that would significantly add to our offering.

We brainstormed as a team, and within weeks I had signed a partnership with the second largest pharmacy chain in the UAE (the largest pharmacy chain thought it was a ridiculous idea!). We built new technology for our front and back-end stacks and integrated Google Maps into our applications. On completing a consultation with Health at Hand, patients could now see their prescription drugs driving towards their home, just like they could see an Uber coming to pick them up. It allowed us to offer things such as at-home urine and blood tests, which were delivered to patients on the back of a motorbike and then taken back to the laboratory for analysis by one of our outsourced drivers.

Not being from an engineering background myself, I was always shocked at the effort required to build new features, both in terms of the cost and of the engineering hours necessary to conclude the work. I did appreciate that this new feature required a rework of our product roadmap, but as the boss I could occasionally pull rank and re-jig the order in which we shipped certain features, sometimes going on my gut instinct alone. Our engineers always found this a challenge and were only really comfortable when they were in charge and had control over the process.

It quickly became apparent that the DHA and local pharmacies had a rather archaic system for how drug codes were communicated and prescriptions were validated. Drug delivery therefore required us to build our own drug codes into our doctor back-end application, meaning we had to effectively build and integrate our own Electronic Medical Record (EMR) system, practically a business venture in itself. Over time our technology platform was becoming more and more 'rich', and I was confident that, if built in the right manner, it would only add to the valuation of the business.

Unbeknownst to me at the time, adding remote prescriptions and the delivery of prescription drugs to our offering meant that we also needed an upgrade to our DHA telehealth license. My regular visits to the DHA's offices restarted, as did my charm offensive. By now I had a better understanding of their processes, and we had some 'champions' within the DHA with whom I had a good relationship.

Once this latest build was complete and the technology was 'shipped', Health at Hand really did offer a best-in-class, full-circle solution where anyone in Dubai could see a doctor within two minutes and thereafter have their drugs delivered to their door (or to a location of their choosing) in under an hour. And since we'd built our solution fast, we'd put some space between ourselves and any other telehealth company that wanted to enter the market, be they another startup or a more established international player.

From a convenience aspect, we witnessed some amazing new use cases, including business travellers who would have a doctor appointment in their taxi on the way to the airport and their drugs delivered to their desired terminal for pick-up before they flew.

By offering pill top-up delivery to patients' homes, we were providing a wonderful new solution for those who were perhaps immobile due to their health or lack of transport. Slowly we were starting to look like a business that even Carlsberg could be proud of.

*

At this point, as mentioned, we were operating a pure B2C operation where all our transactions were between ourselves and individual consumers.

We knew from our research that the major beneficiary of telehealth services elsewhere was in fact the Business to Business (B2B) market, and our desired model had always been to partner with insurance companies who would in turn distribute the Health at Hand app to their thousands of insured patients. This would give us the reach and revenue that we were targeting.

I was acutely aware that B2C businesses were hard to execute and often incredibly challenging to make meaningful revenue from. The cost of acquisition of a B2C customer is notoriously high, not least if you are operating in a new space, as we were. B2C companies often need to invest heavily in brand awareness to build trust and recognition before converting customers and we were no exception, particularly as the first mover. We needed multiple marketing touchpoints to spread the word and educate the consumer base, including media and influencer campaigns, both of which came with high costs. Our low price-point meant that to achieve meaningful revenue numbers, we had to entice thousands and thousands of customers to use our service daily, essentially making us a low-margin, high-volume business. It made complete sense, therefore, to market to the health-insurance companies and target the large patient numbers that they boasted.

Along the way, I had learnt a lot about the pricing of a telehealth solution and come to the following conclusions:

1) Freemium rarely works:

In my opinion, never give away your product for free unless you need the social proof. Complicated or integrated tech products need commitment from your buyer, and asking people to part with some money – even a relatively low amount – often makes that client 'sticky', meaning they have had to think hard before making their initial purchase and are likely to return. We were keen to ensure that any utilisation of the app was deemed as useful by our consumers and that their usage would therefore become habitual.

The opposite of freemium is, in my words, 'reassuringly expensive', and while we never went down this route, there is certainly something suspicious about being offered free healthcare, a hunch that suggests a compromise on quality.

2) Business to Business subscriptions allow you to scale, fast:

Our B2B strategy was to partner with the region's largest health-insurance companies, of which there were only seven or eight. This approach benefited us in several ways. If we could onboard one or more of these health insurers, they would effectively become an extension of our sales and business-development teams as they would have a vested interest in promoting Health at Hand themselves, at their cost.

While we would likely have to drop our prices for a health-insurer client even further, they could in theory unlock thousands for patients for Health at Hand, and this was a much quicker and more efficient route to scale than our initial B2C strategy.

Furthermore, investors love automatic renewal and subscription models. They provide repeatable business and exposure to mass markets.

3) Dual pricing is fine:

We were concurrently running both B2C and B2B strategies and were not afraid to offer different pricing to these two distinct groups of clients. B2C customers were relatively expensive but quick to acquire, whereas B2B took longer but ironically cost less – and we only had the seven or eight health-insurers to impress, so the number of people I needed to market to was significantly reduced.

4) Pricing tech is hard:

Due to the significant financial layout in the upfront build of technology stacks, entrepreneurs want to ensure these fixed costs are covered as soon as possible. But to my mind, if you merely focus on having a positive and growing gross margin, you are on the right track. You don't need to break even immediately.

A gross margin is not the same as profitability, but a positive gross margin does prove that a company is generating more revenue from its products or services than it costs to produce or deliver them. It is defined as:

$$\text{Gross Margin (\%)} = \frac{\text{Gross Profit}}{\text{Revenue}}$$

Investors love to see this number in the double digits (i.e. 10 per cent and above) and growing. The 'growing' bit is important. Even if an investor ultimately wants to see gross margins at 75 per cent (this is often the holy grail gross margin number that investors target for more mature technology businesses), they also love to look at trends. If your costs are tracking downwards and your revenue upwards, you are on a path to profitability, if you haven't got there already.

In my opinion, the gross margin is one of the most important indicators of a company's financial performance. It's the portion of the business revenue left over after you subtract direct costs such as labour and raw materials. In my new post-Health at Hand life as an investor, it's often the first metric I look at in a financial model.

5) Analyse the market:

Map the market constantly. If price is one of your perceived competitive advantages – as it was with Health at Hand – make sure you know exactly what the rest of the market is charging at all times. I did this by constantly using the services of the other international telehealth providers and by regularly testing the different doctor surgeries available in Dubai.

6) Sell on value not cost:

While B2C pricing is likely to be public on your website or app, your B2B pricing is unlikely to be public knowledge. While we were hell bent on trying to undercut the price of visiting a clinic face-to-face, as a business we had to lead with value. What value, above cost, were we providing to the market? If you cannot convince people of the value you are offering, they won't pay one dollar for your service, let alone more. I've worked with businesses that, in meetings with prospective clients, have asked what price the client is willing to pay for the technology. To me, this completely undermines the value you're delivering. It signals a lack of confidence in your product and reveals a fundamental misunderstanding of how pricing should reflect value – not just cost or client preference. And unsurprisingly, when you ask someone what they want to pay, they'll almost always suggest a figure far below what the product is truly worth.

Building a B2B business presents some unique challenges that differ from those in the B2C world, the first being the longer sales cycle and the need to impress multiple stakeholders.

We quickly learnt that, while I was able to access the CEOs of these health insurance businesses fairly easily through my growing network, there were multiple departments within the insurance companies that wanted to be reassured about the Health at Hand business model, and that would be involved in the decision-making and buying process.

I adopted what I called our 'Stakeholder Matrix Model' for each of these large health insurers and began to map which departments and individuals we needed to impress. This often involved extensive online research to identify the members of a company's executive committee – typically the group responsible for making strategic decisions about partnerships with companies like Health at Hand.

On occasion, if the CEO was on board early, he or she would pull together the correct teams internally and introduce me to them early in the sales cycle, saving me a lot of research time. In most cases, however, my business-development strategy involved me analysing who the decision makers were in the CEO's Office, the Finance Department, the IT Department and the Risk and Compliance Department among many others.

I then made it my personal mission to contact and meet all these stakeholders within my target list for each health insurance company, believing that the more senior people I had convinced, the better a chance I had of picking them up as a client. Again, I found LinkedIn a great way of opening doors. Often decisions were made by committee, and if the CEO, the Chief Financial Officer, the Head of IT and the Head of Risk and Compliance had all met me and were convinced by the value that Health at Hand could offer, we had a greater chance of securing a contract when they all sat down to discuss our proposition.

Given the complexity of B2B sales, I was aware that the sales cycles would be long and protracted, but on execution they would often lead to long-term, loyal clients. I knew we had to be patient, and I also knew from my banking days that winning B2B contracts regularly came with additional costs, complexities and technology requirements.

Health insurers on the whole had their own legacy IT systems and would want Health at Hand to integrate our product into these. Any technology entrepreneur will tell you that they strive to build a repeatable product, essentially one that you can resell in the same form to multiple clients, but in the early days it's not always that easy.

In further studying the US and European telehealth markets, we landed on a model where our health-insurance clients would offer our service across a large population of their insured patients, who would then have free access to the Health at Hand application under their insurance plan. Given we were potentially saving our health-insurance clients huge amounts of money by moving patients away from physical doctors' surgeries, their potential cost savings were huge.

Ideally, we wanted all healthcare 'episodes' to commence with a video consultation, where our doctors would act as a triage, but this was perhaps a bit ambitious in the early days. We found that the health insurers didn't want to mandate the usage of telehealth and would rather it be an optional benefit for their insured patients, at least until they studied the outcomes and understood and quantified the cost savings.

We didn't want to risk offering unlimited consultations to patients, and we were worried that a small number of what we called the 'hypochondriac healthy' could clog up our virtual waiting room with incessant requests and questions, thereby blowing our costs out of the water. We therefore determined that insured patients could conduct a maximum of four video consultations per annum for free, paid for by their insurer, but after that we'd treat them as a B2C patient and charge their credit card within the app.

We had access to so much data at this point – data we were, at least in theory, able to share back with our health insurance clients. Data that they hadn't necessarily tracked in the old world. What were the ages and genders of our users? What were the most common ailments we were treating? Were we really reducing the number of prescriptions paid for by the health insurers? What were our wait times, our satisfaction ratings and how frequently did patients return to the app to view their doctor notes?

Data collection was a fundamental aspect of our telehealth app, and we were unwavering in our commitment to collecting and using it responsibly. We dedicated considerable time and effort to ensuring full transparency with our users, clearly disclosing our data collection practices during the onboarding process. It was crucial to us that our customers trusted us completely, and we recognised that safeguarding their personal information was key to earning that trust. We not only met but deliberately exceeded the data privacy requirements set by the DHA. In fact, we went a step further by adopting HIPAA compliance – a practice that wasn't mandated for us but was widely regarded as the gold standard for data privacy in the US healthcare sector. HIPAA, or the Health Insurance Portability and Accountability Act, sets stringent guidelines for the protection of patient health information. In doing so, we showcased our dedication to integrity, trust and the highest levels of data security. On our app and website, we made every effort to signpost our privacy practices clearly, ensuring users were well-informed and therefore confident in the security of their personal data.

In addition to the data we were collecting, health insurers would often want their own unique features built into our product, or for us to remove certain product functionality that they didn't require. This had an impact on our commercial model, and from a pricing perspective for the B2B market, we landed on:

1) A Customisation Fee that would pay for any bespoke implementation work that was required by the client pre-launch. Our health-insurer clients were contractually obliged to pay this in full, up-front, before we did any development work, and
2) An ongoing Subscription Fee for clients to use our service. While we attempted to have these fees paid annually and in advance, the best we could normally manage was quarterly.

Given the volume of clients that these health insurers could potentially offer us, the consumer price per patient was driven down significantly from our B2C offering, but we were comfortable with that; we wanted to build a low-margin, high-volume business for the mass market.

Moving from B2C to B2B necessitates the streamlining of operations, the maintaining of quality at scale and ensuring that your customer service remains robust. Winning a B2B contract would mean that we would have to grow up as a business, and quickly. We would have to meet the stringent data and security requirements of our insurance partners, and we'd have to adhere to their often challenging Service Level Agreements (SLAs) that they would inevitably insert into their commercial agreements.

More than this, we would have to ensure that our B2B marketing was effective and that we provided high-quality, informative content for patients. Consumers would have to know how and when to use the service, and the health insurers would have to be trained to be able to sell Health at Hand to both their current clients at renewal time and to their own corporate prospects at pitch time.

As a team we approached our initial B2B sales meetings with confidence. We had anticipated many of these issues, we had some slick marketing documentation to back our business-case, and we used well-researched examples from other telehealth companies to prove out the huge value that we could offer the market.

Now it was time to knock on doors and try to move from a pure B2C business, with relatively low margins and low volumes, to a B2B business, with even lower margins but much more significant volumes. It was time for us to scale up.

You will recall from Chapter 2 that I had already met a small number of health insurers in the Middle East to canvass their opinion on telehealth at the start of my Health at Hand journey. Now I was excited to return to their offices with a fully cooked telehealth solution that I believed would not only help them reduce costs, but would also assist them in retaining and acquiring new clients. I had listened to their needs and built a product that addressed them.

Many of these health insurers knew that Health at Hand had now launched a fully licensed telehealth solution given that I bumped into them regularly on the healthcare circuit and on my travels – be it at a conference or a DHA roundtable event. I had, however, been quite guarded up until now about how our solution actually worked and what features we offered. I was excited that a small number of these health insurers, it turned out, had come on to the platform as B2C patients themselves, no doubt making up some minor health concern or other to test our offering.

It was time to return to the offices of Christian Gregorowicz, Middle East CEO of the global insurer Allianz's subsidiary Nextcare, a notoriously shrewd operator and someone whom I knew to be incredibly commercially minded. Nextcare controlled a significant amount of the UAE and regional health-insurance market.

Christian was all about increasing revenue and reducing costs, and while patient outcomes and safety were of importance, he was a darling of the global Allianz conglomerate for regularly hitting and exceeding his annual revenue and profit targets. Christian had previously intimated that he understood and liked the telehealth space, but I was convinced that there was no way he had built his own in-house telehealth solution since we last spoke.

I drove to the Nextcare office on Sheikh Zayed Road and entered the lift to the second floor, where Christian's personal assistant greeted me and took me on a tour of the office. 'This is where our marketing team sits, and this is where we manage all our customer-support queries.' It was rather unconventional but indicating great promise to have an office tour during a first formal meeting, and I was excited when Christian finally joined the tour and told me that he had been watching Health at Hand with interest for the last few months and that he was excited to meet again.

Allianz and Nextcare were on a mission to grow their regional market share, and they saw telehealth as one way that they could achieve this. They hadn't built their own solution, nor had they even considered doing so, but they did want to partner with someone in the space so that they could offer telehealth across their large membership base.

Christian was knowledgeable, straightforward and blunt. I enjoyed our interactions, and much like my experience of dealing with Americans earlier in my career, there was no bullshit. He showed little emotion on his face, and I once joked with him that if he weren't a health insurance CEO, he would make a great James Bond baddie!

Before too long, Christian told me that he'd love for Nextcare to conduct their due diligence on Health at Hand with a view to us partnering. We were their chosen regional telehealth provider. This was wonderful news, and on receiving their extensive due diligence pack (twelve documents and over a hundred pages of questions) I re-prioritised my time to focus on getting the most comprehensive answers back to him and his team.

For Health at Hand, Nextcare was what the market calls an Enterprise Sales client – a large organisation requiring a complex B2B sale, characterised by a high level of customisation, extensive negotiations and a strong focus on long-term relationships. By their very nature, Enterprise Sales are often high value and require a considerable amount of due diligence. While some of the questions we were asked focused on our product architecture, much of the detail of Nextcare's due diligence was around our data-security protocols, our systems architecture, how and where we stored our data and how we used patient data.

We were well prepared. Farzal and his team had done a great job in building a technology stack that was appropriate for such a client, one of the briefs that we had given him at the outset. Winning a first B2B client is such a David and Goliath moment. We were undoubtedly the poor partner in the relationship at this stage, and as request after request came into my inbox from Nextcare, we dropped what we were doing to send across comprehensive and appropriately detailed responses.

How could we, a small Dubai-based startup, convince a huge German insurance conglomerate that there was very little risk in partnering with us? This is the challenge for all early-stage companies, and I was consoled by the fact that even the likes of Apple and Amazon would have faced similar obstacles at some point in their history. We worked hard to convince Nextcare that, despite being small, we were a perfectly formed company with all the data and security protocols that they would expect from a much larger enterprise.

Some weeks later we were given the green light from Nextcare that we had passed their due diligence, a not insignificant milestone. It was now time for Christian and I to talk about the commercials of such a partnership. I had considerable negotiating experience collected over my career and prepared by reading Chris Voss's great book on negotiating called *Never Split the Difference*. Chris was an FBI hostage negotiator and not one to pull punches. Great negotiation techniques can make all the difference in closing a deal. One powerful approach is active listening, achieved by truly understanding the client's needs before positioning your offer and presenting your standard sales presentation. Using silence strategically after making a proposal can often work in your favour too, as it encourages the other party to fill the gap and potentially concede. Anchoring, where you start with a strong initial offer to set the tone for the negotiation, is another useful tactic, but in my opinion it should only be used when you have determined a strong motivation to buy. Finally, mastering the win-win mindset and framing solutions so that both sides feel they've gained something helps to build long-term relationships and trust. In all negotiations you should be prepared to drop your price a little so that the other party believes they have negotiated well and achieved even a small win.

I was excited to sit down and see how much revenue I could squeeze out of Nextcare and how many patients we could acquire through our partnership.

At around the same time we knew we had to raise our second round of funding. The timing of the Nextcare negotiations couldn't have been much better. I always think the first round of funding for any business is based on the viability of the team and the vision of the company, but by the second round of funding you need to have proved that the business works, that you have evidenced product-market fit and that you are providing the value you claim you are. To achieve a third round of funding you must back all this up with real numbers – essentially, meaningful revenue and a double-digit, growing gross margin – to prove that you are able to survive and thrive as you scale.

We were raising round two, and a Nextcare contract in my hand was going to be very supportive of a larger valuation.

By this time, we had built what I called our MVP Plus, we had proved the value to the B2C market with some great outcomes (growing patient numbers, high satisfaction ratings, low wait times, etc.), and we were negotiating a commercial deal with one of the world's largest health insurers. Given we hadn't signed yet with Nextcare, but their intent was to do so, I asked Christian to provide me with a Memorandum of Understanding (MOU) for our investor data room. This letter confirmed that Health at Hand had passed Allianz's rigorous due diligence process and that commercial discussions were underway. MOUs are commonly found in data rooms, and companies are more often than not happy to sign them. They provide no guarantee of future business, but they do indicate that there is intent to partner. And it was also in Allianz's interest that we raised money. They liked us and wanted us to succeed. Christian also made himself available for investor reference calls, which was incredibly kind of him, not least because he was one of the busiest men I knew.

One of our original seed investors was representing a large Saudi Arabian family office worth in the tens of billions of dollars. I was invited to fly to Damam in the Eastern Province of Saudi Arabia to meet with their executive team and pitch the Health at Hand story. At the same time, I shared our investor data room with all our original investors and began a series of meetings to try and raise an additional $4 million, which I believed would last us another three years. Raising capital directly or indirectly from your happy-seed investors is much easier than opening new doors, particularly if they are impressed by what they have seen so far.

By now, we were winning numerous awards, and not the ones you paid for by buying an expensive table at an awards ceremony as a guarantee. We were being recognised as innovators, disruptors and game-changers by offering the first localised telehealth solution for the Middle Eastern market. Our solution was based on international standards and quality. Each week it seemed there was more positive news to share with potential investors, and this certainly came at the right time as a huge boost to our investment raise.

Communication was key, and we had recently started two new initiatives to support our brand and reach, both of which I had personally pushed and led on. We began to host regular healthcare events in our own office, hand-selecting industry leaders to both speak and listen to the latest innovations in the sector. This allowed us to produce some wonderful marketing material that fed into our thought-leadership marketing efforts and our soon-to-be released White Paper, the first ever authored in the Middle East for the telehealth industry. We also produced and launched the first of our monthly newsletters, which we called *Pulse*.

Pulse was primarily for our shareholders and prospective shareholders and included a CEO note at the front of each edition, along with an update from Amy, Aftab and Yasmine on their areas of focus, plus some metrics relating to our performance and growth. Thus far, our board had showed very little interest in conducting regular board meetings, and *Pulse* was a great way for me to stay close to them and reassure them of the work we were doing and the progress we were making.

Interest in Health at Hand was also coming from outside of the Middle East, and Allianz's local healthcare partner in India, Bajaj Insurance, began conversations with us while at the same time I also visited neighbouring Iran on the insistence of one of my board members. I knew that partnering with anyone in Iran, be it the government or private sector, would seriously affect our ability to raise money in the future, but nevertheless I loved visiting such a misunderstood and beautiful country and learning more about the healthcare systems of the surrounding region.

Within days of returning from my trip, we managed to hit two significant milestones in our growth. Firstly, we secured the full $4 million investment that I was seeking and closed our Series A investment, with the Saudi Arabian family office leading the round. I still retained control of the business, my stake being now diluted down to about 52 per cent of the share capital, meaning I could ultimately still make all the decisions – advantageous for me and an important consideration given my investors were pretty removed from the business and the developments within the sector.

Simultaneously I executed a thirty-six-month commercial contract with Allianz's regional subsidiary, Nextcare, for Health at Hand, initially meaning that our technology was to be made available to 850,000 patients in the Middle East with a promise of more to follow.

Overnight we had gone from having a handful of B2C customers using the platform each day to having our app in the hands of just shy of one million patients.

Our journey from startup to scale-up was complete. Confidence was at an all-time high within Health at Hand 'Towers'. We had deep pockets, we were on the crest of a wave and we really were dreaming of unicorns.

KEY TAKEAWAYS

- **A competitive advantage is not enough; build a sustainable competitive advantage.** At Health at Hand, while we had no direct competition on Day One, we were keen to build our technology at speed to put space between ourselves and the next mover and were constantly considering how we could retain this advantage.
- **Understand who your consumer is and tailor your pricing accordingly.** We pivoted from B2C to B2B by design and knew that consequently we had to develop a new pricing strategy for each of our different client types. And we made sure to lead our conversations with value and not price.
- **Focus on growing your gross margin.** Gross margins are essential for understanding a company's ability to generate profit from its core operations. Double-digit-and-growing gross margins are a good early target for any technology business.
- **Shoot for the moon. Even if you miss, you'll land amongst the stars.** Set ambitious goals for your business and your employees. Even if you don't achieve exactly what you aimed for, you'll still likely accomplish great things along the way.

8

BLACKBOX MANSION

'Have a healthy disregard for the impossible'

LARRY PAGE, FOUNDER OF GOOGLE

Most technology entrepreneurs will be familiar with the notion of technology accelerators and incubators, but they may not understand the differences between the two, nor indeed how to utilise them to their benefit.

Accelerators are often short-term programmes that help early-stage startups rapidly scale their businesses. Run by third-party companies, they provide things such as mentorship, funding and resources, typically in exchange for equity. Accelerators will generally reward chosen early-stage companies with a place on an intensive development programme culminating in a 'demo day' where startups pitch to perspective investors. These development programmes are designed to 'accelerate' the growth of early-stage startups and typically last between three and six months. Their goal is often to assist in the rapid scale of businesses, to help refine their products or services and to prepare them for market entry or investment.

Within an accelerator, startups will typically have to undergo and pass a rigorous due-diligence and interview process. The selection process invariably involves a deep dive into a company's business model, its market potential, and financial viability. Potential investors and accelerator program managers will assess the founding team's expertise, product-market fit, scalability and any intellectual property or regulatory considerations. The process often includes pitch presentations, technical reviews, and legal and financial audits, certainly for globally recognised accelerators like Y Combinator and Techstars, to ensure the company has the foundation and vision to thrive within the accelerator.

In contrast, technology incubators offer a longer-term, more nurturing environment for startups, often taking them on from the idea stage and providing office space, resources and support over the course of a year or more, without the same pressure to scale quickly. Incubators may or may not take equity, and they often focus on helping startups develop their business models and products. Examples of well-recognised and established incubators include Idealab and Seedcamp.

In recent years, a plethora of accelerators and incubators have been set up inside private-equity companies and even corporates themselves, allowing those corporates to lift the bonnet on several chosen early-stage companies before deciding whether to invest in them or not. HSBC, for example, run several accelerators and incubators for early-stage financial technology (fintech) companies who may be operating in a subsector of the industry that HSBC are either involved in or would like to get involved in. By working with and watching these startups over a protracted period,

HSBC can decide whether to become a strategic investor into these companies.

Both accelerators and incubators offer access to experienced mentors and industry experts who aim to provide guidance on business strategy, product development and market entry. They regularly assist startups with access to a network of investors, potential customers and partners, and may have access to, for example, low-cost legal advice, Microsoft and Google credits or a forum within which companies can share best practices.

Being accepted into a well-known accelerator or incubator can serve as a strong validation of a startup's potential, increasing its credibility in the eyes of investors, customers and partners.

Given Health at Hand had just raised its latest round of funding and had a significant financial runway ahead of us, we didn't need to attract additional investment, so a traditional accelerator was not something we were seeking. I did, however, want to continually improve my own personal skill set and to further develop the high-performance culture that was at the heart of Health at Hand. The learning curve of a founder, and particularly a sole founder, can be very steep in such a fast-paced environment and I regularly felt that I might benefit from some breathing space from the day-to-day running of the business, and some mentorship.

Ever since I left university and immersed myself into the world of business, I have developed a huge interest in Silicon Valley. Having not returned to the US since my auspicious meeting with Pat, I had a strong desire to visit San Francisco again and learn from some of the many successful technology companies operating in California.

In my search for an appropriate incubator, I stumbled upon Blackbox, who actually classified themselves as neither an incubator nor an accelerator but a 'global founder-focused platform that connects founders with the Silicon Valley knowledge, resources and networks they need to succeed'. It was sponsored by Google for Entrepreneurs, now known as Google for Startups, an initiative that provides support to startup communities around the world.

Every three months, Blackbox would reward ten founders of non-US technology companies with a two-week intensive residential stay in the 'Blackbox Mansion' (also commonly known as the Google Mansion) in San Francisco, their mission being to create equality of entrepreneurial opportunity by transforming high-potential founders into global value creators.

Blackbox sounded ideal: two weeks away from Health at Hand to recharge, network and learn from some of the greatest mentors in the technology sector, and a chance to get to know and share knowledge with likeminded founders, who would undoubtedly be facing some of the same challenges and opportunities that Health at Hand was experiencing. If my application was successful, I'd no doubt return to the Middle East with some renewed energy at the very least, but also hopefully some new ideas to help push the business and our team to greater heights, all without giving away any equity.

After completing an extensive online application form and five rather intense video interviews with various young Palo Alto-based entrepreneurs, I was surprised and thrilled to be accepted to join the Blackbox cohort for the fall of 2018.

With my bag packed and ticket in hand, I embarked on one of the most exciting two weeks I'd ever had in my working life.

I arrived in San Francisco having received scarce details about the other nine founders I'd be sharing a house with for the next fourteen days. Blackbox Mansion was located at 711 Scott Street, situated in an affluent residential neighbourhood some two or three kilometres from the city centre. The property overlooked Alamo Square Park, which from its highest vantage point offered wonderful views across downtown San Francisco, including of the famous 'Painted Ladies', a cluster of large, distinctive and brightly painted mansions symbolic of California's mid-nineteenth-century Gold Rush. Blackbox Mansion itself was a grand Victorian mansion some 150 years old, with a typically intricate facade for the period and featuring a towering bay window and detailed woodwork, reflecting the opulence of San Francisco's early wealthy elite. Inside there were high ceilings, decorative fireplaces and wonderful views across the park.

Throughout the first day my new housemates trickled into the property, arriving from various far-flung corners of the world. You could feel the nervous excitement as each new entrepreneur arrived.

The cohort comprised an eclectic bunch of founders. Amongst the gang was Sid, a bright and lively entrepreneur from India with a wonderfully warm smile. Sid was the founder of Wagr, an app for pet parents to track and monitor their furry friends. Garrett, the joker of the pack, had launched his own version of Airbnb for carparking spaces. Based in his native Ireland he had ambition to scale into the US. Carlos, previously Chief of Staff within the Peruvian Ministry of Economy and Finance, had built a business called Quantum Talent that used AI to match people with jobs, and Claire, who hailed from Melbourne, Australia, was founder of VetChat, an app not dissimilar to Health at Hand that connected pet owners with vets via video.

We quickly learnt that the two weeks ahead of us would be full of hard work, wonderful opportunity and no shortage of alcohol. After brushing off the cobwebs of my flight with a gentle jog through the city, I joined the others and we were all greeted in the large sitting room of the house by Fadi, the charismatic founder of Blackbox, and Marie, a young Californian who would be our programme lead.

Fadi oozed charm and confidence and had a quick and brilliant mind. He reminded me a lot of the Hollywood actor Dustin Hoffman. With his quirky, quick and dry wit, and rather frenetic manner, Fadi was immediately likeable and could keep an audience engaged for hours. And importantly, he was highly thought of in nearby Palo Alto where the great and the good of the technology-investment world plied their trade.

Fadi had established Blackbox to disrupt the traditional accelerator model, having previously been founder and CEO of techVenture, a successful recruitment firm that focused on venture-backed high-growth startups in Silicon Valley. Originally from Syria, he also did considerable work to help 'accelerate world peace through entrepreneurship', working with organisations such as Startups Without Borders and VIP Fund, a social impact fund investing in innovative technology and education solutions to connect youth globally. In the breaks between the afternoon sessions, Fadi would pour me or one of the other guests a glass of red wine and enquire about the challenges we faced within our businesses, or simply share stories of his own startup journey, or fascinating tales of his family and his upbringing.

Sessions generally ran from early morning until mid-afternoon and covered a diverse range of topics. One morning, we might listen to a guest speaker explaining how to influence consumer behaviour through digital marketing. On another, a data-focused session might feature a guest lecturer introducing third-party software tools for potential integration into our own technology – to track metrics such as session duration, the total time a user spends in an app during a single visit.

Each session was announced by the song 'Take Five' by Dave Brubeck being pumped through speakers situated in all corners of the house. This allowed us five minutes to collect our things and gather our thoughts before each session started. Quite rightly, if you showed up late after such a protracted starting gun you were considered to have let the group down, and we each bought into the mantra of being 'present' throughout the programme. In essence this meant not only turning up for each session on time, but always engaging fully, with mobile phones off and brains on.

There were certainly uncomfortable moments for me, particularly in the first few days. A culture of inclusiveness and caring could in my mind occasionally spill into one deriving from Silicon Valley's sixties hippy roots, and I did not immediately take to our morning ritual of holding hands in a circle, meditating as a group for two minutes, before going round the room and enquiring of the person to your left, 'How are you doing today?' and, 'Is there anything I can help with?' I struggle to think of a bigger cultural divide between this environment and the one on the Morgan Stanley trading floor.

Claire, Elize and I were a rare breed amongst the group in that we were married with children and a little bit older than the others. Having a not dissimilar background to myself, Claire and I gravitated towards each other when doing group tasks in the early days and we empathised with the demands placed on each other as both sole-founders and parents, occasionally sneaking off to check-in with our respective businesses and families back home.

As the programme went on my respect and warmth towards each of my housemates grew considerably, without exception. Louise was assertive and passionately feminist, with a huge ambition and a work ethic to match; Elize was quirky and not afraid to speak her mind; Yannik was inherently cool yet openly and honestly wore the scars of a previous technology failure; Alex was kind, gentle and thoughtful; and Marie was relatively guarded and introverted but with a sharp wit. Each of us brought something unique to the group and to the sessions, and, importantly, we all had our own challenges, flaws and success stories to share, acquired during our quest to become technology billionaires. Throughout the fortnight, I shared special moments with each of my new friends, learning an immeasurable amount from how they were building their businesses, and from their own personal aspirations and values.

I have always been rather sceptical about traditional methods of education, where all are required to study the same curriculum in the same manner, irrespective of each pupil's personality or goals. This view of mine stretches from schooling all the way to the likes of master's degrees, which I believe to be on the whole incredibly impractical, prohibitively expensive and far too theory-based. My own master's degree was still in progress, attained through the setting up and running of my own business; from 'doing' rather than studying. There is no substitute for learning on the job, and Blackbox was a great complement to everything I was trying to build as a sole founder.

I was fortunate that my cohort felt comfortable sharing their experiences, offering guidance, and supporting me in a way that was truly unique. I remain grateful for their trust and friendship, even though we now only catch up from time to time through our WhatsApp group.

Each afternoon, we'd be coached by the inimitable Bill Joos in the basement of Blackbox Mansion. His role was to help each of us hone our forty-five-second 'elevator pitch' and to refine our three-minute business introduction so that we'd use our time on stage wisely during the final evening's investment pitches.

Articulating your business in a clear and concise manner is an absolutely crucial skill for a founder. Three minutes is not a long time, but it's a great exercise to be able to communicate the who, the what and the why in such a short period of time.

Bill was a large chap with an even larger character marked by a warm-hearted kindness that drew people in despite his boisterous demeanour. Born in North Dakota, he had started numerous companies in the first half of his career before launching his 'Go To Market Consulting' business which focused on business plans, modelling, messaging, presentations and strategies. Sadly, he has since passed away, with his obituary in *The Mercury News* accurately noting that 'his zest for life and an infectious smile brightened the lives of everyone around him'.

Bill worked us hard each day, forcing us to think differently about our businesses through a range of solo and group activities. He frequently gave us evening homework to complete overnight which we'd be required to share with the group the following day. He gave structure to Blackbox. His daily sessions were interspersed with inspirational talks from local investors, seasoned founders and Fadi himself, who would frequently coach us on the challenges we were likely to face as our businesses developed.

Each evening, we were all required to report to the main sitting room area, where we would have supper as a group on the long dining table. Even these events were incorporated into a part of our networking and learning experience. Three of our group would be responsible for cooking each night and would have to turn up one hour earlier to prepare a feast for the group. This was a brilliant idea and allowed us to get to know each other better and to enjoy each other's company. If it was your night to cook, you'd arrive in the kitchen to a fridge full of the ingredients for the evening's feast and a recipe laid out on the kitchen island.

The best part of these evenings occurred each night at 8 pm on the dot. It was then that a special guest would arrive, just as the food was being served. Often these guests would be famous and often hugely successful names from the technology scene in San Francisco. I must admit that my housemates were often much more aware of who they were than I, having seemingly read many more books on entrepreneurship, but it was with huge excitement that we opened the door each evening to our dinner party guests.

On one notable evening we were joined for dinner by Adam Cheyner. Adam was someone whom I'd never heard of by name, but I certainly knew his work. He was co-founder of Siri Inc, the digital assistant now built into each Apple iPhone, iPad and Apple Watch. A rather shy and awkward conversationalist, Adam's story was fascinating, and I was desperate to ask him several questions. Being on cooking and serving duty that evening, I was unfortunately sat at the opposite end of the table to Adam, and I was frustrated that I was unable to hear much of his conversation or ask his advice.

The nightly ritual saw the full Blackbox team waving our guests off at about 10 pm in an Uber, not wishing to lean on their time or generosity too much, after which we'd invariably continue drinking until midnight or beyond, playing games or simply hanging out.

On this occasion, and no doubt on the back of an inspirational day of entrepreneurial learning sessions, I decided I wanted more time with Adam. On an impulse I asked him how far his home was from the Blackbox Mansion as his Uber pulled up outside.

'At this time of night, it should take me about forty-five to fifty minutes.'

I doubled down, and proceeded to ask if he'd think it strange if I offered to accompany him on his journey home and then turn the Uber back to return me to Alamo Square? On reflection I think he did find it a little unconventional, but my bravery was rewarded with a forty-five-minute one-to-one with one of the great minds of Silicon Valley in the back of his Uber. Adam was open, kind and incredibly generous with his contacts and the insights he shared with me during that night-time taxi ride. Having risked overstepping, I felt my bravery had paid off. He paid for my return ride, offered up his own personal email and mobile number and, true to his word, he introduced me to a handful of interesting connections over the subsequent few days. As I have said, if you don't ask, you don't get, and I tend to find that people are often much more generous that we might imagine.

Twice each week we'd have a night out with Marie chaperoning us to one or more of the trendy bars of San Francisco, often accompanied by a gang of Blackbox 'friends' made up of previous participants on the programmes, acquaintances of the Blackbox team and mentors who were connected with the programme. We'd visit the bars of Valencia Street in the Mission District, a vibrant hub for young professionals seeking post-work relaxation. Lined with eclectic bars and eateries, it offered a bohemian atmosphere that reflected the area's artistic heritage.

San Francisco's night life was varied, and we'd normally end up in Polk Steet, where venues ranged from the creatively themed Kozy Kar that celebrated 1970's car culture to dance-friendly spots like Rouge that showcased a different up-and-coming DJ from the San Francisco music scene each night of the week.

While I was there, San Francisco was high on its reputation as the world's most progressive city when it came to technology and entrepreneurship. Meanwhile, the global technology-investment scene was marked by several major themes that were shaping the direction of venture capital and innovation:

1. The Emergence of AI and Machine Learning

Artificial intelligence (AI) and machine learning were two of the key emerging themes during this time, particularly in areas like natural-language processing and predictive analytics. The excitement around AI was driven by its potential to disrupt various industries, from healthcare to finance. While my own knowledge of this space was woefully inadequate at the time, AI and machine learning were the huge buzz words in Silicon Valley, and it seemed that the wider world only caught on a few years later.

2. Blockchain and Cryptocurrencies

The explosion of interest in blockchain and crypto currencies, specifically the likes of Bitcoin, was a defining trend. Initial Coin Offerings (ICOs) were surging in popularity as a new fundraising method, raising billions of dollars, despite regulatory uncertainties.

3. Growth of SaaS and Cloud Computing

Software as a Service (SaaS) and cloud computing continued to be dominant themes, with investors keen on businesses offering scalable, subscription-based software solutions. As a business, we were cognisant of this and were tweaking our own business model at Health at Hand accordingly. Companies focusing on enterprise software, data analytics and cloud infrastructure were attracting significant funding.

4. Expansion of Fintech

Fintech was seeing massive growth, with investment pouring into areas such as mobile payments, digital banking, lending platforms and insurance tech. The rise of fintech was driven by a shift in consumer preferences towards digital financial services and the need for innovation in the financial sector. We were the beneficiary of this trend with multiple choices when it came to the integration of a mobile-payment solution into the Health at Hand app.

5. Autonomous Vehicles and Mobility

Investment in autonomous vehicles and the broader mobility sector was another significant trend at the time. Elon Musk, whose company Tesla was at the heart of this sector, was one of the few entrepreneurs with global name recognition. Companies working on self-driving cars, electric vehicles and related infrastructure (like charging stations and mapping technologies) were drawing substantial interest, fuelled by their potential to revolutionise transportation, and while many were still sceptical about the safety aspects, this was another exciting space to be involved in.

6. Healthtech and Biotech

Health technology and biotechnology were also gaining traction, with investors focusing on innovations in personalised medicine, genomics and digital health. Doctor on Demand in the US, Babylon Health in Europe and many others were beneficiaries of significant investment from venture capital and private equity as technological advancements were seen as a transformative force for improving patient outcomes and reducing costs.

7. China's Growing Influence

During these years, China was also beginning to emerge as a major player in the global tech investment scene, with significant venture-capital activity and the rise of Chinese tech giants like Alibaba, Tencent, and Baidu. Some of the investment focus had shifted from Silicon Valley to China, not least because of the large investment amounts that the Chinese were prepared to commit.

On the flipside, however, there were concerns over technology-company valuations and talk of a potential market correction. Technology companies like Uber and Airbnb had relatively recently received huge investment sums despite being far from profitable. Investors had up until now been willing to commit funds based on the significant growth potential in top-line revenue without much concern for the ultimate profitability of the businesses they were investing into. In many cases, these businesses were not only years away from returning a profit but had no idea when they'd even break even. Investors and analysts began to worry about the sustainability (or not) of such high valuations, particularly in the context of the unicorn startups. Had they been valued too high, too early? Given my banking background and my desire to build Health at Hand for exit rather than for lifestyle, I watched this theme with interest and was aware that a focus on bottom-line growth was ultimately going to be much more highly valued than pure top-line growth.

Against this backdrop I was incredibly excited for what we had heard was one of the highlights of the Blackbox programme: a day trip to Palo Alto to meet some of the great and the good of the investment community. Palo Alto is considered the birthplace of Silicon Valley and is home to some of the earliest technology companies, including the likes of Hewlett-Packard, which was founded in a garage there in the 1930s. Stanford University was another Palo Alto darling, often credited as being a major catalyst for the growth of Silicon Valley, fostering innovation and entrepreneurship through its engineering and business programmes.

One of the huge advantages of Blackbox was the programme's ability to unlock doors, and we were certainly not disappointed when Fadi announced we would be having private meetings with senior partners from renowned investment houses such as Kleiner Perkins, Sequoia Capital, Venrock and Norwest Venture Partners. Senior partners of these firms rarely even met the CEOs of the companies that they invested into, so for us to have an audience with them was both very exciting and a little daunting.

Randy Komisar from Kleiner Perkins was a hero of mine. He was advisor to and investor in some of the great names of the technology scene and was also co-author of books such as *Straight Talk for Startups*, which provides actionable advice for launching and scaling a successful startup, *Getting to Plan B*, on managing innovation, and *I Fucking Love that Company*, on building consumer brands.

As we introduced ourselves in Kleiner Perkins' oversized boardroom, delivering the forty-five-second elevator pitches Bill had helped us craft, Randy looked nonplussed. It was apparent that in the US they think big, and we learnt that Randy (and indeed most other local investors) needed to believe that every company they invest in has the potential to become a unicorn. On sharing our future-growth ambitions (e.g., $5 million revenue by year three or $20 million revenue by year five), Randy seemed concerned. Add another zero or two to our projections and he'd likely have looked more interested. Randy's notion was that in a portfolio of say twenty technology investments, at least fifteen may fail, four may have moderate success and the one unicorn will carry the performance of the whole investment strategy. We came across as fledgling technology businesses, operating in markets too small to be of interest to him. He did however offer each of us some sage advice, impressing upon us the need to think much bigger. It was a huge coup to have an hour of his time, and I left his office both inspired and intimidated.

As the day progressed, courtesy of Blackbox, we had the privilege of meeting some more of the most influential and active investors in the global technology ecosystem, featuring names instantly recognisable to us such as Andreessen Horowitz, Accel Partners and Benchmark Capital. My Blackbox colleagues and I were frequently shocked by the numbers being bandied around in Palo Alto, and we collectively came away with a desire to multiply our ambitions by 10.

A quirky tradition at Blackbox was that the group would return from Palo Alto in an alcohol-fuelled limousine complete with nightclub specification speakers. Our fortnight was coming to a close, and in a sense this was our cohort-ending party, providing us with the opportunity to let our hair down. I remember crawling through the rush-hour traffic on our return to Alamo Square, arm in arm with my new friends as we screamed 'Mr Brightside' by The Killers at the tops of our voices from the comfort of our blacked-out limo.

The lingering effects of the previous day's hangover were quickly overshadowed by my desire to make a strong impression at pitch night, and we rose early and spent hours fine-tuning our presentations, rehearsing every detail to perfection. Like so many accelerators, the Blackbox programme concluded with a chance for its participants to showcase their vision. Each of us ten entrepreneurs was required to present our business for three minutes to a room full of some of Silicon Valley's most successful and discerning investors. While many in the cohort were nervous, I was excited by what lay ahead, perhaps given I had more experience of presenting to large and intimidating audiences than others. Throughout the programme it had also been made clear to us that historically very few Blackbox businesses had secured funding during Pitch Night, and so my expectations had been managed. This did not concern me at all; Health at Hand was by now well capitalised, and I wasn't in the US on the false premise of raising capital that I didn't need. I was there to learn and grow, and in that sense the trip was everything I'd wanted and more.

By the time early evening rolled around, the once-empty basement room of Blackbox Mansion had transformed into a buzzing hub, filled with dozens of local technology influencers, investors and entrepreneurs. The energy in the air was electric, and the camaraderie among we participants was almost tangible as conversations sparked across the room, blending excitement with a shared sense of purpose.

There was a real sense of connection, trust, and mutual support between me and the nine other founders. We had all been brave and driven enough to start our own businesses. We'd been vulnerable enough to share our personal challenges with each other over the last two weeks, and while we were all perhaps suffering from a sense of imposter syndrome, we'd all come so far and had grown so much together during the fortnight we spent together.

As I expected, Pitch Night provided no investment for any of the group, but new friendships had been made and we all left feeling much richer for the experience. It was an absolute privilege to have participated in the exclusive invitation-only 'club' that is Blackbox, and my respect and admiration for the other founders could not have been greater.

Clutching my own personal affirmation book that each of my Blackbox cohort had filled with words of encouragement and praise, I returned to the Middle East with renewed energy and a whole bunch of ideas that would hopefully inspire my colleagues as we embarked on the next phase of the business.

KEY TAKEAWAYS

- **Technology accelerators and incubators can be fantastic, but . . .** Research the options well and determine what they can do for you rather than what you can do for them. You don't have time to waste two weeks or more of your entrepreneurial journey, so make sure you select on value and not vanity.
- **Don't be afraid to ask.** Asking Adam Cheyner if I could accompany him on his journey home was a risk, but what's the worst that could have happened? He could simply have said no, which wouldn't have been the end of the world. I find that if you ask in the right manner then entrepreneurs, and people in general, are more inclined to help than you think.
- **Technology valuations are not what they used to be.** The world has changed and no longer can you raise investment based on top-line growth alone – you must have a clear pathway to break-even and profitability.
- **Americans think big.** It's a fine balance between over-egging your numbers and being seen to have a lack of ambition. But if you want to attract US investment, you need to think big!

9

THE HONEYMOON PERIOD IS OVER

'There is no education like adversity'

BENJAMIN DISRAELI

Since studying the theory of company evolution, as part of my university education, I had been aware of the different growth stages of a business, namely: 1) Existence 2) Survival 3) Success 4) Take Off, and 5) Maturity.

Health at Hand had successfully navigated stages 1 and 2, and on my return from the US I predicted that we were somewhere between Stage 3 and Stage 4 – a huge achievement given so many companies fail before making it this far. Signing our enterprise sales agreement with Nextcare before my trip was a significant inflection point, providing a strong sense of validation that we were on the right track. I was also aware that the skill of a founder, and indeed their leadership team, is to keep the business in Stages 3–5 for as long as they can.

In both life and business, success is often the precursor to unexpected challenges. It is not uncommon to experience what can best be described as a false dawn – a fleeting moment of triumph that is soon followed by adversity. Within the business world, the term 'hockey-stick growth' is frequently invoked to describe the trajectory that every company aspires to achieve. This term refers to the visual representation of exponential progress on a graph, where key metrics rise steadily before surging upwards. Almost every investment proposition showcases graphs that climb from the bottom left to the top right of the page, painting an appealing picture of unrelenting success.

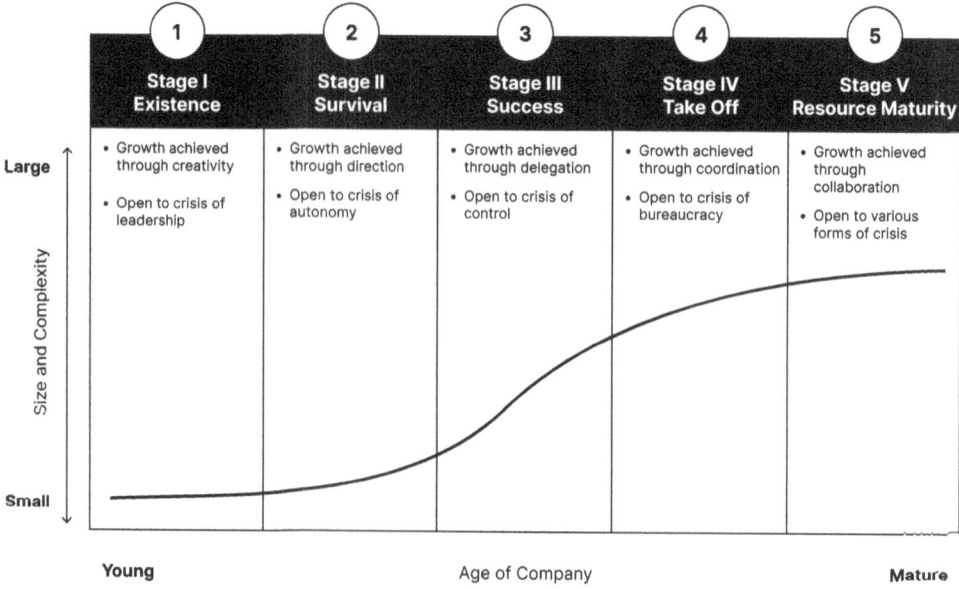

For a significant portion of our journey, this narrative appeared to hold true for Health at Hand. If one were to chart our growth in terms of user numbers, revenue or client acquisition, the resulting graph would undoubtedly resemble a hockey stick. It appeared our momentum was unstoppable, and we were frequently bashing down the few obstacles or speedbumps thrown at us along the way. This upward trajectory was achieved with relatively minimal input from my board or external advisors, save for Nadim. Nadim stood out as a rare and invaluable asset; his insights were profound, and he truly grasped the essence of what we were striving to build.

Nadim's contributions, while significant, were certainly not the sole drivers of our success. Health at Hand thrived because of a combination of factors: a dedicated team, a clear vision and an unwavering commitment to innovation. Yet success, when experienced too swiftly, can sometimes mask underlying vulnerabilities.

Reflecting on this period, I am reminded of the importance of balance in scaling a business. While celebrating wins is essential, it is equally critical to remain vigilant and prepared for potential setbacks. The allure of a flawless upward trajectory can sometimes blind even the most seasoned entrepreneurs to the complexities and inevitable challenges that come with sustained growth. Our story thus far, though punctuated by moments of triumph, served as a testament to the resilience and adaptability required to navigate the peaks and valleys of the entrepreneurial journey.

Soon after I returned from the euphoria of San Francisco, we encountered our first significant challenge. We were currently relying heavily on Farzal's highly accomplished Karachi-based Next Generation team, but despite their proficiency they were geographically distant and somewhat detached from our business in their working practices. If we wanted to be a success in the long term, we had reached the stage where I felt it necessary to foster a team that was embedded within our organisation, sharing our workspace and immersed in our product and culture. A co-located team would build stronger communication, deeper collaboration, and a more profound sense of ownership over our product. It was a calculated risk, but one that aligned with our mission to build a company rooted in a shared purpose and mission. In my bid to gradually transition our tech team from being entirely outsourced to an in-house, Dubai-based team employed directly by Health at Hand, I had devised a strategic approach. Each time we required a new technology employee, we would hire in-house in the hope that over time a seamless migration would occur.

The responsibility for this shift of focus was on me, and I never regretted it for a single minute; but I did, however, quickly regret the first hire we made as a result of this decision.

Given the growth of our user numbers and the fact we had recently launched across Android to complement our iOS application, we determined that we needed to hire an additional Android developer. I was keen to hire someone who was not only highly skilled and experienced, but was already working in the telehealth sector, believing that they would bring with them new skills and insights to the business that we didn't already have. A symptom of telehealth being a relatively new concept was that we had limited direct telehealth experience across the team, and I wanted to redress this balance.

I tend to consider it dangerous to have too many pre-requisites when hiring, and by limiting our search to only those working in telehealth, I was aware that the pool of candidates would be much smaller. We were, however, living in a time when telehealth was rapidly expanding, particularly in the Western world, and fortunately, we were not short of applications for the role.

On the face of it, Dimitri was the perfect hire. A lover of motorcycles and tattoos, definitely not pre-requisites for the role but fun hobbies all the same, he was currently working in the UK for an established telehealth company, who we had regularly studied as a management team along with ten or so other global telehealth companies that were on our radar. Having tested their app on numerous occasions myself, I was pretty impressed with its User Experience (UX) and User Interface (UI), and I admired how they had generated so much publicity in the UK, despite what we suspected were still relatively low patient numbers.

Given my lack of engineering expertise, the team, including Farzal, were responsible for determining if Dimitri had the right skills to perform the job. Where engineering interviews were concerned, Farzal would ordinarily design a forty-five-minute engineering task bespoke to each role. He really cared about the integrity of the process, providing extensive feedback on each candidate and spending considerably more time on each hire than I expected him to.

Our high-performance culture meant that I also needed to be convinced that the successful candidate could also add something to elevate the current team, and by the time Aftab passed Dimitri's recruitment file across to me for his final 'cultural fit' interview, he had persuaded a sufficient number of the team that he was up to the task. Farzal was a great help during the whole interview process, and indeed whenever we had any human resources-related challenges. He shared my desire for ensuring that each new hire would help us grow as a business. His willingness to support us was even more admirable given it meant we might, in time, reduce our reliance on his own outsourced team.

Dimitri interviewed well both from a technical and a cultural perspective and was duly hired. In addition to his salary, we paid for his flight from the UK and a relocation allowance, which included two months of paid-for rent in a nearby serviced apartment.

Aftab and Dimitri hit it off immediately, despite coming from wildly different backgrounds, Dimitri hailing from Athens and Aftab, Lahore. I was pleased to hear tales of them going out for dinner together and attending the odd concert during the early weeks of Dimitri's employment in Dubai. I am a big believer that if someone's life outside of work is in a good place, they are likely to be a better colleague and friend, and I did as much as I could to ensure Dimitri settled into his new life in the Middle East, including hosting a barbecue at my villa for the whole team during his first week.

It wasn't long, however, before there was trouble in paradise. Only days before Dimitri was to reach the end of his three-month probationary period with Health at Hand, a letter was emailed to me from a lawyer in the UK. Having never managed my own company before, I was unaccustomed to receiving such letters, and I opened the attachment with a degree of concern. Health at Hand were being accused of stealing some of the technology code from his former employer. We were asked to evidence the specific code we had stolen and to provide details of where we had integrated it into our own technology. The lawyers requested that we immediately undertake a full audit of our technology platform, performed by an independent and reputable technology consultant and paid for by ourselves.

Ouch! This was a first for me, and while over the course of my career I had been involved in some difficult decisions, including redundancies and the closing of regional offices, this was a dagger to the heart. We had built Health at Hand to be a bastion of good practice with a moral compass to match. I was hopeful that this was a Dimitri issue and not something that involved other members of our team. Had he indeed integrated some of their code into our own, and if so, was anyone else on the team complicit? I invited Dimitri to join me in the office boardroom to discuss the situation.

As a sole founder, there are times when democracy works well and you benefit from canvassing the opinion of others, but there are also times when you must make decisions yourself, in isolation. This was one of the latter. I absolutely wanted to give Dimitri the benefit of the doubt, believing in the innocent-until-proven-guilty principle, but I also had a responsibility to Health at Hand and, indeed, Dimitri's former employer. If he had stolen code from them, it was a complete breach of everything I and the business stood for.

To give him some credit, Dimitri moved from a position of denial to one of guilty admission and compliance within a matter of minutes. It turned out that he had indeed saved some of his former employer's code on a personal file when he left the business, stupidly leaving a trace of this activity on their server when renaming the file 'Health at Hand'.

While he insisted that, thus far, he had not accessed the file, I owed it to all parties to conduct a thorough investigation. My immediate action was to suspend Dimitri on full pay while we investigated the matter.

Our internal investigation first involved interviewing all our engineering team, and thereafter I asked Farzal to conduct a thorough exercise to determine if there was any errant code within our own. We then paid an independent technology consultant to conduct their own investigation, which was no small matter, given it required a fairly detailed understanding of both of our businesses, and came with a fee to match.

Not feeling the need to hire lawyers ourselves to respond, I wrote back to Push Doctor and told them that I took their letter extremely seriously, that we believed the breach to be down to their former employee Dimitri, not Health at Hand, and that we believed that their code had in no way been used to advance our own product. I let them know that we would send them the findings of the independent audit within the next three weeks and that Dimitri had been suspended with immediate effect.

The upshot of the investigation was that Dimitri had indeed stolen some code, but that, as he himself had protested, none of this had filtered into the Health at Hand product. Additionally, none of our other employees were involved or even aware of Dimitri's actions. With hindsight, the legal letter had arrived in a timely manner, and the repercussions could have been much greater a few weeks further down the line.

When looking back on this episode I am proud of how decisively I acted. Despite the understandably accusatory tone of the legal letter, suggesting we were complicit in stealing their code and using it to our own benefit, the outcome was a cordial future relationship between our two companies. I did have to ask Dimitri to leave the business, but given that he had only recently relocated from the UK to Dubai, and the fact that I am a believer in second chances, I personally introduced him to a number of recruitment friends and asked Aftab to keep an eye out for him.

In reaction to this episode, we hastily rewrote our employee handbook and added some additional clauses to our employment contracts to cover any similar events in the future. There is no shame in continually improving your processes and learning on the job, and we were reactive in the face of a challenge we had not anticipated.

I was conscious that this whole incident might have an adverse effect on our engineering team's morale. Dimitri had behaved poorly, but we were a small team, and I decided to get on the front foot to try and ensure we moved on quickly.

Motivating a team after letting someone go requires thoughtful and deliberate leadership, as the loss can have a profound impact on the team's morale and ability to move forward. To address this challenge, I implemented a comprehensive four-pronged approach, designed to tackle the situation head-on and rebuild trust within the team.

Firstly, I prioritised being open and honest in my communication. Transparency was essential to help the team understand the reasoning behind the decision, so I carefully explained that while there were lessons to be learned from Dimitri's departure, the decision to let him go was made with respect and the broader interests of the business in mind. This candour laid the groundwork for a renewed sense of trust and encouraged openness.

Secondly, I took the opportunity to foster resilience within the team. I emphasised that while change can be unsettling, it also presented a chance for growth and innovation. By shifting the focus to our future goals, encouraging the team to focus on our shared aspirations, I aimed to unite everyone around a common purpose and instil a sense of collective responsibility, helping to ensure that the culture remained strong even in the face of transitions.

I also attempted to reignite the team's excitement about Health at Hand's vision by reminding them of the critical role each individual played in our growth and success. This emphasis on the future helped to redirect energy away from the negative emotions surrounding Dimitri's departure and towards a renewed sense of purpose and collaboration.

Thirdly, I made a concerted effort to support colleagues who were directly impacted – particularly the engineers and Aftab, who had worked closely with Dimitri. I recognised that they had not only lost a colleague, but also a friend. By providing them with the space to express their feelings and concerns, I fostered an environment of empathy and understanding while encouraging them to work together to overcome the transition.

Finally, I took the time to acknowledge and celebrate the hard work of the entire team. Recognition is a powerful motivator, and by highlighting their contributions, I hoped to rebuild morale and inspire confidence in our collective ability to move forward. This recognition was not only about boosting spirits, but also about reinforcing the value of their efforts within the organisation.

These actions were critical in allowing us to move past this challenging period and in maintaining the team's morale. By addressing the situation with transparency, empathy and a focus on the future, we were able to foster a sense of resilience and unity, ensuring that the team remained motivated and aligned with our shared vision. In the following few weeks, I also made a point to check in regularly with certain individuals who I perceived to have been adversely affected by the incident more than others, reassuring them that their contributions were valued and that our commitment to a supportive work environment remained unchanged. One conversation that stood out was with Aftab, who had forged a personal friendship with Dimitri. I reassured him that Dmitri's actions were in no way a reflection of the great job that he was doing and that he should fell very secure in his role within the business.

At around the same time, other challenges slowly started presenting themselves to the business. Given our patient volumes were on the rise, we were fearful that our business would now be on the radar of the Telecommunications and Digital Government Regulatory Authority (TDRA), who monitored all telecommunications within the UAE.

The UAE, along with the wider Middle East, was extremely guarded when it came to telecommunications. Geographically, the UAE is surrounded by a hotbed of politically instability, with countries like Syria, Saudi Arabia, Lebanon, Iran, Iraq, Pakistan, Yemen and Afghanistan in close proximity. There were often rumours that the UAE residents were having their mobile phones monitored by the TDRA, and the use of applications such as Skype and Zoom was at the time prohibited.

Health at Hand's business model required us to have Voice over Internet Protocol (VoIP) capabilities embedded within our app. Given the regional restrictions when it came to third-party communication applications, we initially decided to build our own VoIP platform, engineering a proprietary video code on top of the Web Real-Time Communication (WebRTC), which enables applications to capture and stream audio and video media.

The TDRA were on the prowl, and we were concerned that at any moment they could shut down the business if they were concerned about our telecommunication tools. Middle Eastern government entities had an authoritarian style, and if they didn't like something, they'd normally act quickly and decisively, without asking too many questions.

In my usual tenacious style, I decided to get ahead of any potential sanction from the TDRA and sought a meeting with their leadership team. I am always a believer that being proactive is far better than sitting back. But in this instance, I failed dismally. Despite the determination with which I attacked the issue, I could not for the life of me find a contact to meet within the TDRA. The DHA were equally unsupportive and were unwilling to provide me with a letter to confirm that they were comfortable with our business model – despite the fact they had obviously licensed us as a business and that we were proving out our business model.

Not wanting the government to stop us trading without warning, we decided to integrate a back-up VoIP provided by a third party called TokBox. It wasn't that the TokBox solution was formally approved by the TDRA either – it wasn't – but I thought it was prudent to have a Plan B if they were to ever voice their concern over our Plan A.

We relaxed somewhat when this fall-back solution was in place, but the reality was that in the Middle East you never really knew when you might be hit with a sanction or a fine. However, hoping that the government might have more important priorities than to sanction an early-stage telehealth business, we finally felt like we could put the issue to bed.

As our business grew, so did the level of government and public scrutiny, making it clear that we needed a more structured approach to identifying and managing risks. The landscape felt increasingly precarious, with new regulations, compliance requirements and operational challenges emerging rapidly. It was at this moment that we decided to build a risk register for the business, again reacting in real time to the challenges we were facing in our desire to continually improve the business and how we operated. I had used risk registers in previous roles before to plot threats, assess their impact and put mitigations in place. We determined which risks we believed we faced as a business, canvassing the opinion of the full team – alongside which we included actions as to how we might remediate them. With hindsight we should have done this sooner, but it's never too late to begin something so important.

A risk register ensures that potential threats are proactively identified and addressed, and by consolidating risks in one place, it allows teams to anticipate and prepare for potential challenges. A well-maintained register also helps leadership make informed decisions by prioritising the mitigation of risks based on their likelihood and potential impact. Without one, companies risk being caught off-guard by unforeseen events, which can lead to significant operational or financial setbacks.

Our own risk register soon became an integral part of our monthly leadership meetings and quarterly strategy sessions and allowed us to make proactive decisions. Within a relatively short period of time, we had identified a vast number of potential threats to our business, not uncommon for a company operating in the healthcare sector. It could at times seem overwhelming, given we'd resolve one issue only to uncover three more, but alongside each challenge, we built detailed plans and timelines for how and when those risks would be addressed. It gave me great peace of mind that we were acknowledging these concerns head on and not hiding from them, and it allowed us to reprioritise some of our day-to-day activities.

But there were some challenges beyond my work life that could not be accounted for in this way. While I had returned from San Francisco with renewed energy and vigour for the business, I was conscious of being pulled in multiple directions by both Health at Hand and my family, who were in the process of relocating back to the UK. We believed rightly or wrongly that the UK education system was better suited to our children than the education Dubai had to offer.

Claire and I had now lived overseas for twelve years, and as expatriates we had benefited from a transformative, horizon-expanding experience. Living in both Asia and the Middle East, we had been gifted the chance to immerse ourselves in new cultures, languages and to develop a deeper understanding of the world. It had challenged our adaptability, pushed each of us out of our comfort zone and enabled us to build resilience and problem-solving skills. The experience had not only exposed us to different perspectives and undoubtedly broadened our worldview, but had fostered an empathy and appreciation for diversity that we perhaps didn't have before. Building relationships with people from varied backgrounds had enriched not only our social circle, but brought a huge sense of adventure and excitement.

Despite the many wonderful benefits we had enjoyed during our time in Dubai, and the fact that all three of our children were born there, it ultimately made sense for Claire and the children to return to the UK ahead of me. The decision was not an easy one, but it was practical given our circumstances. The plan was for me to join them in the UK as soon as the demands of the business allowed. However, at such a critical stage for Health at Hand, I simply could not step away from my responsibilities.

During this period, I quickly achieved Gold Card status with Emirates airline's loyalty programme, a silver lining that afforded me access to the business lounges at both ends of my frequent journeys, despite flying economy. Additionally, thanks to my consistent travel, I was often fortunate enough to be upgraded, which slightly alleviated the strain of long-haul flights. Nevertheless, I often found myself yearning for the generous travel budgets I had enjoyed during my time with HSBC and Shuaa Capital, which had made such trips considerably more comfortable. This chapter was marked by both sacrifice and determination, driven by a commitment to both my family and the business.

In the preceding weeks, work had consumed more of my energy and focus than I would have preferred, diverting my attention from my family. Frequent travel accompanied the demands of building the business, but the true challenge lay in the mental strain of juggling these responsibilities. As an involved parent, I had always prioritised attending my children's sports matches, school plays and concerts. While my family remained at the forefront of my priorities, there were moments when I felt I was falling short in my commitments to them.

There were times when I felt dejected by the conflict of these competing demands, but I was consistently lifted by my family's unwavering support for my pursuit of this potentially once-in-a-lifetime opportunity. Their encouragement reminded me of the importance of seizing this chance, while balancing my role as a parent.

Many early-stage companies undergo a mass hiring programme following a funding round, but Health at Hand still had a relatively lean team. I had so far not felt the need to add too many more people to our headcount. I frequently witness founders who will use their swollen bank accounts as an excuse to hire executive assistants, CRM leads and multiple new salespeople without considering how each of these new hires will each fill a forty-plus-hour working week. It is not uncommon for such an environment to lead to a round of redundancies some months down the line when the realisation dawns that the new team members are not additive to the growth of the business.

I did, however, believe that we'd reached the stage in the business's growth when hiring a strong 'number two' to support myself had become essential. As companies expand, the demands on the CEO's time and energy grow exponentially, often making it challenging to maintain focus on both the strategic vision and the operational details. Bringing in a competent second-in-command, such as a Chief Operating Officer (COO), would allow me to divide responsibilities effectively. My aim was for this new hire to oversee the day-to-day operations, enabling me to concentrate on our long-term strategy, investor relations and driving innovation.

Moreover, I was hopeful that the new hire would be able to introduce fresh perspectives, potentially identifying opportunities and solutions that we might have overlooked thus far. I was proving to be a competent frontman and a good door-opener, and by now I was widely known and respected across the region as a trusted and authoritative voice on all things telehealth, but I needed a more office-based COO who would ensure that we didn't drop the ball on our core activities.

One skill of successful founders and CEOs is knowing which skills are required by the business and which they are personally lacking, and in building out a job description for the role, I conducted an exercise mapping my own personal strengths and weaknesses alongside the skills I believed the business needed.

I was confident that any new hire would not only enhance our organisational capacity, but position Health at Hand for sustained growth and scalability, while reducing the risk of leadership burnout.

Fortunately, our recruitment drive unearthed one stand-out candidate. Sameer was a serious operator and someone with an extensive background in healthcare and telehealth. A speaker of multiple languages, Sameer was ten years younger than me and a qualified doctor. Immediately prior to Health at Hand, Sameer had been Head of Medical at a large regional healthcare group, and he had lived in and around the healthcare sector all his life, his

THE HONEYMOON PERIOD IS OVER

father being a well-respected doctor in the region. On a personal note, I managed to determine that Sameer was unmarried but had a long-term girlfriend and what seemed like an incredibly stable family life. In his interviews he came across as being thoughtful and driven, and we were absolutely delighted when he accepted the role as COO as he would bring real and recent experience to the role.

Bringing Sameer onboard as a supportive and capable right hand was a great and well-timed move, and Sameer, alongside Aftab, remains one of the hires I am most proud of across my whole career. Sameer made an immediate impression and was quick to take the lead in various operational aspects of the business, including ensuring our licenses were up to date, managing our doctor onboarding and scheduling process, and liaising closely with Aftab to ensure we honed the consumer side of our application.

I was conscious that Sameer was our first new senior hire for some time, and despite his thoughtful nature, I was keen to make sure that his occasionally assertive and combative style didn't upset the status quo of the team or have a negative effect on our culture. He would now sit alongside Yasmine, Amy, Aftab and I in our leadership meetings, and I was keen to ensure that he promoted a positive environment within the business.

Sameer was not afraid to tell it like it was, and I was grateful for his candid approach. As a leadership team we prioritised several key areas to ensure Sameer's smooth integration into the company, focusing on alignment, collaboration and maximising his impact. First, we emphasised cultural onboarding, making sure that Sameer fully understood the company's values and norms. Starting from the interview process and continuing into Sameer's first few months with the business, we clearly communicated the essence of our organisational culture, encouraging him not only to embrace and buy into it, but also to contribute to its growth in meaningful ways. This created a foundation of mutual respect and understanding.

We also worked to manage his assertiveness, recognising that Sameer's fresh perspective and direct communication style could be transformative for the business. We encouraged him to voice his ideas confidently while aligning his confidence of thought with a culture of collaboration and respect. This approach set a clear expectation that his contributions, while bold, would complement the team's dynamics.

To support this, we promoted open dialogue as an ongoing practice. By fostering a culture of regular feedback, we ensured that both the leadership team and Sameer could share insights, express concerns, and adapt to changes seamlessly.

With these new guardrails in place, Yasmine, Aftab, Amy and I immediately warmed to Sameer, welcoming him with open arms into the leadership team. He breathed life into the business, inspiring us all to elevate our game a little given his strong work ethic and his commitment to improving our operations.

As all good COO's should, Sameer quickly drove several operational efficiencies across the business. Among his other areas of focus, he worked brilliantly with our doctors to devise and manage their shift patterns. Sameer's appointment didn't afford me a quieter working life, but it did allow me to focus more on raising our next round of funding, analysing our competitors and sustainable advantages, determining which new features and products to roll out and keeping Health at Hand front and centre in the health-insurance market – while further advancing our relationships with the various health regulators across the region.

In short, Sameer focused on the day-to-day while I focused on the future.

The investment landscape in the Middle East at the time was one of large boasts and even larger cheques. Babylon Health were purportedly doing great things in Europe, and soon after Sameer's appointment, I found the time to make a trip to their London headquarters to learn more about their artificial-intelligence-led diagnostics tool.

Babylon had been making huge headlines, not least because they had received $550 million in funding from the Middle East's largest investor, Saudi Arabia's Public Investment Fund. It was difficult not to get excited at such numbers being invested into a telehealth company, or at their valuation at the time of just over $2 billion. I was aware that if we could stay on top of what companies like Babylon were doing in other markets, and if we could continue to keep ourselves in their thoughts, we might become an acquisition target for them further down the line, and I was not afraid to speak candidly and directly about this to Babylon's CEO, Ali Parsa, when I met him.

As an entrepreneur, there are some areas of your business and the market that you can influence, and some areas where you simply have no say. Often, the most successful technology companies, the unicorns, have an element of luck to their stories where the headwinds seem to blow in the right direction, carrying them to great things. Timing is everything, as the phrase goes.

Conversely, you won't always have a smooth ride, and it was around this time, and completely out of the blue, that Abraaj Capital, the Middle East's largest private-equity firm came crashing down when a whistleblower exposed a black hole in their finances.

Abraaj managed about $14 billion in assets across the emerging markets, with a bias towards healthcare. Their CEO was the charismatic Arif Naqvi, who was alleged to have misappropriated circa $250 million. Investors in Abraaj's healthcare fund, including the Bill & Melinda Gates Foundation, had raised concerns about the misuse of their monies, helping trigger the firm's demise.

This felt quite close to home. I had met Arif on several occasions, and we had even shared a stage on a panel just a matter of weeks before at a regional healthcare summit. The news sent shockwaves through not only the investment houses of the Middle East, but more specifically, the healthcare sector. The whole story was subsequently covered brilliantly in Simon Clark and Will Louch's book *The Key Man*, which provided a commentary on how the global elite were duped by Arif and Abraaj. Raising future finance in the healthcare sector was going to be a challenge against this backdrop and, in my mind, there was a heightened urgency for Health at Hand to scale cross-border and become profitable before we were required to raise further funding.

The mood across the UAE felt heavy. It seemed the outside world was questioning the valuations of regional companies as well as the competence and professionalism of regional investors. And there was collateral damage, as Abraaj's fall took some smaller investment companies down in its wake over the next few months. Given the huge growth that cities like Dubai had experienced in the previous few years, with many commentators questioning its sustainability, Abraaj's fall seemed like a line in the sand and a 'we told you so' moment, with many outsiders revelling in the body-blow Dubai was experiencing.

As Christmas approached, I was excited to have a flight booked to the UK for three weeks to spend some much-needed time with

Claire and the children who were doing a great job of settling into UK life.

But not before tackling another challenge that had recently hit my desk.

As I had feared when trying to counter the TDRA, I eventually fell foul of UAE's notoriously fine-heavy regulatory bodies. Each year in mid-December, the DHA, along with other UAE government entities, would customarily issue fines to companies.

While I was out visiting clients, Amy received a visit to our office from some DHA officials. We were being asked to pay a fine of AED 100,000, the equivalent of about $27,000. To this day, despite having the Arabic documentation translated into English, I still don't know exactly what the fine was for, the paperwork being particularly ambiguous. Nevertheless, our lawyers advised us that it would be cheaper and easier in the long term if we just paid it and moved on, and we duly obliged. It was so frustrating, but we were always cognisant of the fact that we were pioneering a novel business in an emerging market and that we were pushing boundaries. It was never going to be easy, and while I hoped that our first-mover advantage would benefit us further down the line, we knew there would be speed bumps along the way.

Looking back, we'd faced a challenging few months, with various curve balls thrown at us. As I flew out of Dubai, I jotted down some notes on what I'd learnt personally during this period and what we collectively as a business might do better next time. I was happy that we had been extremely transparent in our internal communications with our team, in our external comms with our investors and stakeholders and that we had built a strong sense of purpose and resilience across the business, something I later termed 'innovation under pressure'.

With the fine paid and a green light from the DHA to continue operating, I left the business in the safe hands of Sameer for the Christmas period.

KEY TAKEAWAYS

- **Act decisively.** There are times as a founder when canvassing the opinion of others is not necessary, and you should go with your gut. I remain proud of how I handled our legal challenge, suspending Dimitri immediately, undertaking an immediate investigation and communicating professionally both internally and externally.
- **Keep a risk register.** It was only due to our fears of shutdown following our implementation of VoIP that we began to keep a risk register – but it is never too late to begin this process. It is always important to track and grade the risks to your business on an ongoing basis and to close any gaps through action. There will always be some risks that you cannot control, but for the others, work hard to find a solution.
- **Don't hire for the sake of it after a funding round.** Frivolous spending won't help the business. Be disciplined and focus on hiring the team you need and not the team you want.
- **Worry only about what you can control and influence.** Abraaj Capital's fall from grace was not our fault – but we did show resilience in the face of external challenges, and we fostered a culture of 'innovation under pressure'.

10

THINGS START TO UNRAVEL

> 'The road to success and the road to failure are almost exactly the same'
>
> COLIN R DAVIS

Our partnership with Nextcare was going well. Having originally launched Health at Hand across 850,000 of their insured clients in the UAE, I had pitched to their regional management team to see if we could expand this contract across their wider Middle Eastern client base, and without too much additional work we had reassurances that we would win an expanded mandate to cover up to four million patients that Nextcare managed across the six countries of the GCC.

Expanding a current contract is always easier than winning new business, and having passed Nextcare's due diligence some months before, Health at Hand were already an 'approved vendor', meaning that we appeared on their internal system as one of their global procurement partners. Allianz and Nextcare's decision-making process was much easier this time around, meaning that the regional head of their business in Bahrain, for example, had very few hoops to jump through to get the Health at Hand service approved and up and running in his country of focus.

We had always had an ambition to scale the business cross-border, and given we were still operating a low-margin business, we were forever brainstorming as to how we could increase patient numbers. Scaling across multiple countries with one client was a huge coup, and I set Amy to work in ensuring that the news was heard far and wide, particularly by the handful of competitors that were by now beginning to spring up in the region.

Expanding into multiple countries is not a simple process though. There were a number of areas of the business that we had to consider in operating outside of our original market of the UAE, and I established a sub-working group within the business so that we were appropriately prepared for this additional work.

As a team we analysed in detail what we believed to be the five most pressing areas of interest and risk, and made sure no stone was unturned as we prepared for our multi-country expansion:

1. Market Research

We believed we had a considerable knowledge gap in some of the countries we were expanding into, and we set about understanding the needs of the local customers, regulations and competition. It was absolutely crucial for us to understand the motivation to buy our services in each of these new countries if we were to make a success of this expansion. A resident of Kuwait might have completely different healthcare needs and demands than someone in

Qatar, for example. Our growing history of consultations allowed us to track trends through the data we were collecting, and residents of Kuwait at the time had a high prevalence of lifestyle-related diseases such as obesity and diabetes, often requiring a focus on preventive care and chronic disease management. In contrast, Qatar's rapidly growing expatriate population was seemingly driving a need for more specialised services, including mental-health support and family health programmes tailored to diverse cultural backgrounds. It was important that we weren't lazy in the way we approached our research and that we didn't make any unsupported assumptions. It was clear to me that scaling was not just a copy and paste exercise. We revisited the consumer workshops we had done prior to launching in the UAE market and tried to find out as much as we could about our new customer base, including how to localise the service we were offering where possible.

2. Regulatory Compliance

While the UAE was often regarded as a standards-setter for the region when it came to healthcare regulation and compliance, each country in the GCC has their own healthcare regulations, their own equivalent of the TDRA and their own insurance companies who come with their own set of unique KPIs. We reminded ourselves continually that we were operating in the healthcare sector and being compliant with local regulations was a non-negotiable for a business of our type. We worked hard to understand the nuances of the regulatory landscape in these new and different markets. I found that each of the countries we were expanding into had a government-led business unit whose sole purpose was to help foreign companies operate in their market. I sought out these business units and with mixed success they each offered up some advice, with the Bahrain Economic Development Board and Invest Qatar being particularly helpful.

3. Cultural Differences

Despite the UAE being a hotbed of cultures, there has always been a willingness of the population of the UAE to conduct their business in English. Even Uber, by now one of the country's most widely used applications, was yet to translate their app into Arabic. But across the wider GCC, this wasn't necessarily the case, and in some regional countries conducting business in English was frequently frowned upon. We therefore took a decision to re-language our apps into Arabic and at the same time, French, hoping that we might at some point expand into the likes of Lebanon and North Africa. From a technology perspective it made sense to add these two languages at the same time and it meant we wouldn't need to re-visit this activity for a while.

4. Hiring Local Talent

We considered hiring local, in-country teams, or at least an individual for each new country in which we were operating. We debated whether someone with local expertise would be able to help us bridge knowledge gaps and win new, non-Nextcare customers. On reflection, I decided that it was a little premature to do so. I was also fearful of hiring a single local managing director in, say, Oman until we were a little bigger, as he or she might be too far removed from the heart of the Health at Hand UAE business. I was happy in the interim to take on the responsibility for these additional markets myself, and I prepared myself for spending even more time on the road and in the air.

5. Infrastructure and Operations

Finally, we knew we had to establish reliable IT support systems to ensure we could operate efficiently cross-border. This included a re-architecture of our data storage capabilities, with many of our new Nextcare clients requiring in-country storage. This in itself was no small task, and after an initial planning stage we had to reconfigure much of our Amazon Web Services (AWS) architecture and ensure our regular performance, security and risk standards were met through optimisation testing. For many of our clients, this was a pre-requisite to conducting business in a new country, so again, it was work that we would benefit from further down the line.

While expanding into new countries had been a dream of mine from the moment I founded Health at Hand, I was also aware of the risk of 'overtrading', the scourge of many companies bigger than us. Overtrading occurs when a business takes on more work than its resources – such as cash flow, inventory, staff or operational capacity – can handle. I was conscious that Allianz and Nextcare were still in the driving seat when it came to the commercial side of our relationship. It was obvious that at this stage of our growth, we needed them far more than they needed us, and they, of course, were smart enough to know it themselves, something that was reflected in their relatively aggressive contract negotiations and the subsequent commercial terms we had executed between us.

I was acutely aware that if our operations and customer-support functions became overwhelmed at any point, our customer-service standards would inevitably suffer – an issue I was determined to avoid. Upholding our reputation had been a priority of mine from the beginning, and I had consistently championed its importance within the organisation. Witnessing the continuous stream of positive feedback to our customer support team was not only rewarding but also a testament to the team's commitment to excellence, a source of enormous pride.

At the same time, I was resolute in ensuring that the Nextcare expansion would generate a modest profit for the business in its own right. While I recognised our relatively weak negotiating position, I also understood the value Nextcare placed on our service and partnership. It was essential to me that we resisted the temptation to treat the Nextcare account as a 'loss leader' by offering our services at below-market rates simply to secure the business. I needed to focus on the long-term sustainability of the business, and by striking the right balance, we could safeguard both our reputation and our profitability.

Loss-leader strategies are commonly used in the retail sector to drive foot traffic or increase brand loyalty. Supermarkets might offer discounts on staple items, like bread or milk, selling them at a loss in the hope that customers will enter their store and also buy other products sold at greater margins. Such a strategy can backfire if customers only purchase the discounted items. In our case, this would reduce our ability to become profitable and given Nextcare were by far our largest client, we needed to be careful.

I was also aware that the Nextcare expansion brought significant advantages beyond just financial gains. Partnering with such a reputable company was beginning to also give Health at Hand invaluable publicity and enhanced brand recognition, which further elevated our profile in the market. Each time I saw Nextcare promoting their

Health at Hand partnership in the media, I couldn't help but feel a sense of satisfaction. The deeper Nextcare's involvement was with Health at Hand, the more secure our partnership seemed, making it less likely they'd ever want to walk away.

It wouldn't have been fair to say that Nextcare was our only client at this time – we had a handful of other B2B clients, as well as our direct-to-consumer patients, who were still paying out of their own pocket for Health at Hand's services – but we did have a growing and pressing issue: Nextcare's contract size as a percentage of our total revenue had grown even larger with this new cross-border agreement, and they now represented an unhealthy 80 per cent of our total revenue.

There is always a danger of being over-reliant on one client, and it can present risks to a company's survival if not addressed, given the financial vulnerability it introduces. If Nextcare were to reduce their spending in the future, or even worse, switch to a competitor, we'd have a big problem on our hands. My research showed that for more mature companies than Health at Hand, it is commonly acknowledged that no single client should account for more than 15–20 per cent of a company's total revenue. We needed to win non-Nextcare business quickly in order to redress the balance so that the fate of the company was not tied disproportionately to the actions and decisions of Nextcare alone. If our Nextcare relationship were to encounter any issues, replacing the lost income quickly enough to cover fixed costs, payroll and operational expenses would be a huge challenge.

When a large client dominates revenue streams, it often shapes the company's product offerings, their processes and overall strategy. Thus far, much of our engineering time had been spent on ensuring our product was a fit for Nextcare, rather than being fit for the wider market. As a management team, we knew that the optimum scenario for a SaaS company was to build a repeatable product that we could sell to multiple clients in the same form, with little or no refinements as we expanded. An off-the-shelf solution was our goal, but it seemed that satisfying the unique demands of Nextcare was consuming an inordinate amount of time and energy, making it difficult to accommodate other prospective clients who all had their own requirements.

Another major challenge of Nextcare accounting for so much of our revenue was the loss of negotiating power when Christian and I sat down to discuss the expansion. He knew full well that they were our largest client, and this put me in a weak bargaining position. I cannot attribute any blame to Nextcare – they were making the most of the situation as it presented itself – but their smart negotiating was proving hard to rebut and I was conscious that the results could be damaging for us further down the line.

Maintaining negotiating power is crucial for the long-term financial sustainability of a business. It is common in the early stages of a business for the pricing power to sit with your prospects and clients – in other words, they can call the shots. As we expanded beyond Nextcare, we would need to ensure that our margins increased, and I believed that we had the product and the team to navigate a course to calmer waters.

The other issue with single-client dependency is that investors just don't like it. Client concentration limits a company's diversification, both financially and strategically. I was very aware of the perceived risk the investment community would highlight in the case of Health at Hand and Nextcare. Investors will always favour a diverse revenue stream across a diverse client base. Diversification provides security and softens the blow if one client is to take away their business at short notice.

While we still had some runway ahead of ourselves, so there was no need to panic, there were several horror stories relating to other companies in the back of my mind. One such story was that of BlackBerry, makers of the handheld device that preceded the rise of iPhone and Android devices. In its early years, BlackBerry had a major contract with Verizon Wireless, which became its largest client. While this relationship provided substantial revenue during its peak, BlackBerry's over-dependence on a few large carriers limited its ability to innovate as quickly as the competition when the smartphone market grew. When carriers like Verizon and AT&T shifted their focus to iPhone and Android devices, BlackBerry struggled to recover, ultimately resulting in their dramatic decline.

Another example is Nortel Networks, a telecommunications giant that collapsed partly due to their over-reliance on a small number of large clients. When a few of Nortel's key customers reduced orders and delayed payments during the early 2000's tech downturn, Nortel experienced severe cash flow problems, leading to their bankruptcy.

Companies that diversify their client base tend to navigate downturns more effectively. Amazon Web Services (AWS), despite being a dominant player in the cloud computing space, had at the time a broad client base across various industries, preventing it from being overly reliant on any one customer. Their diverse client portfolio allowed AWS to remain resilient even as different sectors of the economy faced volatility and as competition to their product emerged.

There was no obvious silver bullet for Health at Hand. We were a new company operating in a new and emerging subsector of healthcare, and not everyone wanted to adopt our technology at the time.

As a result of my concerns, I re-prioritised our insurance pipeline and focused on those companies we believed wanted to be leaders in innovation as opposed to those happy being followers. Who perceived our technology as a must-have as opposed to a nice-to-have? Sometimes, regardless of how good your sales pitch is, the people in front of you just aren't ready to buy.

I also came up with three additional ideas for mitigating our over-reliance on Nextcare and began to explore a few new initiatives including:

1. New Markets

With Nextcare as an anchor client in a number of new countries, could we use them as a springboard to attract other companies to partner with us? Nextcare did not have exclusivity, and I was in theory able to speak to all their health insurance competitors.

2. Expanding Our Product Offering

Were there new products or services that we could develop to allow us to appeal to a wider audience and thereby reduce our dependency on Nextcare? Again, I set-up a sub-committee internally to explore some other ideas which if successful would not only diversify our revenue from a client perspective, but also from a product perspective.

3. Client Retention and Growth

Could we increase the business we were doing with our other current partners so that their revenue became more meaningful? We had recently signed a relatively modest partnership with a small hospital group in the UAE. Was there opportunity for us to expand this contract further and into other areas of their business?

The over-reliance on Nextcare continued to be an open item on our risk register and not something we were hiding from internally. The important and unanswered question for me was why had Nextcare decided to roll-out Health at Hand across the full region, yet the other insurers were yet to follow suit? Were Nextcare more progressive than their competitors and therefore willing to include technology-led solutions within their insurance plans before their rivals were? Did Nextcare have a different business model to the rest of the market, one where the Health at Hand solution really benefited them in a way that wouldn't necessarily apply to other insurers? Had we neglected some of the other insurance companies in our business-development outreach or struggled to get in front of their key decision-makers?

It sounds obvious, but the best way to find answers to these questions is to actually ask, and I conducted another round of meetings with the significant insurance companies in the region, where possible arranging face-to-face meetings with their leadership teams.

My conclusion was that the market not only liked our product, but they loved the Health at Hand brand, and the employees that they had met, whether it was me in sales and strategy meetings, Aftab during product demos, Sameer discussing the integration of our technology into their platforms or Amy articulating how we would educate and inform their insured members.

The core issue, as we identified it, was that both we and Nextcare were somewhat ahead of our time. While regional insurers recognised the significant advantages of technology-driven solutions, their decision-making processes were, for the most part, cautious and conservative. Budget constraints further limited their willingness to immediately engage in a commercial partnership with Health at Hand. Many of these insurers fell into the 'watch and wait' category, preferring to observe how Nextcare leveraged and benefited from our solution before committing themselves.

Understanding this dynamic, it became clear that our primary objective was to ensure that we remained front-of-mind for these more hesitant players. By staying visible and demonstrating ongoing success through Nextcare, we could position ourselves as the logical partner of choice when these more conservative insurers decided the time was right to adopt a similar approach.

Throughout my career I have constantly returned to the notion of 'motivation to buy', be it for a banking product or Health at Hand's technology platform. Despite me attempting to convince the market that Health at Hand was indeed solving some of the real problems it was facing, winning a new client seemed like it might require some patience.

Despite our relatively lean team, our net outgoings at the time were about $150,000 per month. Given that revenue growth was also slow, I knew we needed to extend our runway by raising more capital. I had secretly hoped that we'd have broken even, or be at least close to breaking even, by this time, but with Nextcare squeezing us on our margins and our struggles to onboard any new meaningful clients, we needed more time.

Notwithstanding the investment backdrop of Abraaj Capital's demise, I was still confident that we could raise two to three years of additional capital, in all likelihood our last ever capital raise before becoming a profitable business able to stand on its own two feet.

I needed to breathe a little more financial life into the business. I reflected on myself, questioning my own resolve and determination to continue the journey, and concluded that I absolutely still had the energy to conduct another round of funding negotiations.

It was time to build another investor data room – but this time the documents had to be even more compelling than before.

When a company wants to raise capital, one of the most critical tools at their disposal is an investor deck. As a business we had already been through this process twice, and fortunately I enjoyed both building the investment documentation and the subsequent process of presenting these documents to the investor community.

Given Health at Hand was now a few years old, and we had already launched our product on the market, the expectations for the quality of our investment documentation would be high. We were no longer raising capital based on an idea or a concept. While investors would obviously be interested in our prospects, they'd also be concerned with how we'd spent the money thus far, how we had translated this money into commercial contracts and when we'd become a profitable business.

To put it simply, an investor deck is a presentation that outlines your company's mission and vision, your business model and your financial projections, all with the aim of convincing investors to provide funding. It should be a succinct, high-impact document that grabs the attention of potential investors and communicates key aspects of your business in a way that is both clear and compelling.

In my view, an effective investor deck should come in two forms: a short-form 'Pitch Deck', which acts as a teaser and tries to weed out those investors who are just being inquisitive from those who actually have a real interest in your business, and a long-form document, often called an 'Information Memorandum' (an 'IM'). These documents serve different purposes in the fundraising process, but both are crucial for attracting and impressing investors.

The 'Pitch Deck' document was something I always sent to my investor community first, and I'd happily email this to people without the need to sign a Non-Disclosure Agreement (NDA). As such, our Pitch Deck only included headline information and not the full detail that an investor would ultimately require to make an informed investment decision.

I designed our new Pitch Deck document to give a quick yet compelling overview of the business with a maximum of twelve slides. The goal of our Pitch Deck was to generate enough interest to either secure a face-to-face meeting or for the interested party to sign an NDA and receive the more detailed IM.

While some think that an NDA provides friction in the fundraising process, I prefer to see the signing of an NDA as affirmation that there is serious interest to see more. NDAs themselves often don't serve the legal purpose they are designed for – to protect confidential disclosures – and some venture capital and private equity investors will simply refuse to sign them, but for me they are a step in the process that dictates a certain level of interest over just curiosity.

I was keen that our documents were visually engaging, concise and easy to understand. Fortunately, at Health at Hand, I was blessed with a great designer in Shiju, and we were always able to present aesthetically pleasing documentation with our brand's DNA running through everything we produced.

The key slides we included in our Pitch Deck were:

Introduction slide: This is the 'Who are we?' and 'What do we do?' section. I was reminded of the workshops I had conducted in San Francisco as part of Blackbox, where I was taught to clearly articulate the 'who' and the 'what':

> Health at Hand are a market-leading telehealth business, allowing patients to access primary healthcare wherever and whenever they need it through our proprietary iOS and Android apps, connecting them remotely with US Board Certified doctors within a matter of minutes, while at the same time providing a cost-containment tool for the health insurance market.

Problem and Solution slide: This is an incredibly important slide and one which I find many entrepreneurs often forget to include. Don't just say how brilliant you are – tell the reader why your product or service is a necessity and convince them that people will pay for it. Here I was clear to mention how Health at Hand solved a meaningful problem for patients (convenience), for insurers (cost-containment) and for healthcare regulators (providing primary-healthcare access to mass populations). In this section I included several screenshots of our product to bring the story to life. These would also hopefully emphasise that we were not in the conceptual phase; we'd actually launched and were thriving.

Market Opportunity slide: Investors are ambitious, as I had discovered in Palo Alto. They want to know that the market is substantial and that your business has a chance of capturing a significant share of this market. Here I included the market research we had conducted to define the total addressable market (TAM), the serviceable available market (SAM) and the serviceable obtainable market

(SOM), all of which are important metrics well-understood by the investment community.

Whenever I used an external data point (for example: the global telehealth market is set to grow from $1 billion in revenue to $2.5 billion in the next twelve months), I made sure to include a source for that data and a direct link to where I had obtained the information. Creating trust and credibility with investor prospects is important, and the process is helped by providing well-researched data points.

Business Model slide: It is within this slide that I began to sell the financial story of Health at Hand. Investors need to see that you have a clear and scalable business model. I outlined our current wins and future-growth projection, being careful not to make overly optimistic and plain stupid assumptions about how quickly we would expand. Forecasting with excessive optimism can sometimes get you laughed out of the room before you've even met your prospective investors, so again everything needed to be well-researched and realistic.

Go-to-Market Strategy slide: Here I discussed how I planned to acquire and retain customers. I described our acquisition strategy, our marketing channels, our sales tactics and our partnerships. Our Nextcare regional expansion really helped to enhance the presentation, a proof point that there was demand for our service beyond just the UAE, and I asked Christian to provide a quotation to back up what a great company we were to work with.

Competitive Landscape slide: In this slide I identified our competitors and alongside them I articulated our differentiators. Investors frequently ask about the competition and rather than hiding the fact we had others now playing in our space, I thought it best to get on the front foot and call them out early. Investors want to know that you are both aware of the competitive environment and have a strategy to stand out and win. I used a SWOT analysis (Strengths, Weaknesses, Opportunities and Threats) chart to add credibility and detail.

Traction slide: Here I really tried to show off about our Nextcare partnership and also shared other early successes and milestones, such as our revenue growth, customer-acquisition growth and a roster of our clients and partnerships, as well as a section on our product-development milestones and our technology roadmap. Investors are more likely to back companies that have demonstrated early signs of success, and while we were not quite where I wanted us to be, we had much to be proud of.

Financial Projections slide: Within this slide I included a high-level financial forecast for the next five years, which incorporated the revenue, costs, profit margins, and key financial ratios. While investors don't expect perfect predictions, they do want to see that you've thought about growth realistically. Supplementary to this, I built a much more comprehensive and dynamic financial model in Excel to be shared only once an NDA was signed. This file included formulas so that investors were able to stress test our assumptions. As is common with many financial forecasts, I outlined three potential growth projections across a number of different metrics: 1) conservative 2) moderate/expected and c) aggressive.

Team slide: This is another slide that I feel often gets missed or is not presented as well as it might be. Investors want to know why they should back the key individuals behind the business. I was keen to highlight our leadership team and their relevant experience but also the credentials of our brilliant doctors. Investors invest in people as much as they do in ideas, so the aim here was to showcase why our team was uniquely positioned to execute the plan and bring the business to life.

Investment Ask slide: In this slide I clearly stated how much capital we were seeking and how we planned to use the funds. Investors want to know how their money will be used to generate returns and a breakdown of your spend across various functions such as engineering, product, sales and marketing can prove really useful.

Conclusion slide: I was keen to end with a strong closing statement that reiterated our value proposition and the opportunity at hand. Essentially this was a 'why us?' and 'why now?' slide. If an investor had read this far – they rarely do – my conclusion was a call to action:

> If, like us, you believe Health at Hand and the telehealth sector provides a great investment opportunity, please do email to gain access to our full data room.

As stated earlier, a Pitch Deck is designed to pique investor interest, an IM to my mind should be a much more in-depth document and typically shared only after initial interest is established. It should provide investors with a comprehensive view of the company, including its risks, its financials and some detailed strategies.

Health at Hand's IM was a document of between twenty and thirty pages. The key difference to the Pitch Deck is that I ensured it was bespoke to the reader. Given that anyone who reached this stage had already shown serious interest, I could then study their websites to get an idea of which sectors they were interested in, what other investments they had made and what they looked for in an investment partner before I shared with them the IM. I'd make sure to add their company logo to the front cover, and when we met, I'd show off my knowledge of their company to highlight my research. If you cannot even find time to research your prospects before a meeting, how the hell can you convince them that you are the right people to partner with.

In addition to the slides I had included in the Pitch Deck, there were a handful of more detailed slides that I included in our IM:

Executive Summary slide: Containing slightly more detail than the Introduction slide in the Pitch Deck, my executive-summary slide included an overview of the business as well as Health at Hand's mission, vision and values and some key highlights.

Market Research and Analysis slides: Here I included a deep dive into the market in which we were operating, including a detailed breakdown of the market size, growth trends, customer types and competitive analysis. I'd hopefully impress the reader with all the proprietary research we had done as a company, including our user-persona work, our consumer-behaviour findings and the details of the consumer workshops we'd conducted along with their conclusions. This section could run to two or three slides and was very data-driven and well-researched to build the client's confidence in the business and opportunity.

Product Detail slides: These slides provided an opportunity to show off about our engineering team, details of how we build our product, which features we had shipped and what our product roadmap looked like for the next two to three years.

Detailed Financial slides: These slides provided more detailed financials than the Pitch Deck, including cashflow projections and our projections for breaking even, as well as some headline metrics such as gross margins and how they were set to improve over time.

Operational Plan slide: I included a thorough explanation of how the business operated day-to-day. This covered how we managed technology sprint cycles, our customer success function, product-development processes and key partnerships, with a particular focus on how we managed doctor and patient queuing and onboarding. I wanted to impress upon potential investors that we had built a solid foundation for scaling our operations.

Risk Factors slide: Every investment carries risks, and it was important for me to be transparent about ours. This section outlined the potential risks as we saw them, such as market shifts, competition, legal and regulatory issues and execution challenges – plus, importantly, how Health at Hand planned to mitigate these risks. Here my focus was primarily on regulatory risk and malpractice risk, which we considered to be our two greatest daily challenges.

Use of Funds slide: Investors need to understand how their money will be used. This slide provided a clear breakdown of where the investment would be spent, whether it was on hiring, product development, marketing or other operational costs. Investors are reluctant to see too much money going into salaries, particularly those of the founder(s), and would rather the money was being spent on a) building a real product with a re-sale value, and b) winning new business.

Exit Strategy slide: Investors are naturally focused on understanding when and how they will see a return on their investment. However, contrary to common belief, many are willing to exercise patience – particularly those who have identified you as ideal long-term partners. It's not always necessary to promise immediate or medium-term returns. Instead, the key lies in tailoring your messaging to align with the priorities and expectations of the specific investors you're engaging.

In my approach, I customised the exit-strategy section based on insights gathered during discussions with potential investors. I outlined realistic exit opportunities – including acquisitions, an initial public offering (IPO) or stock market listing, or secondary market sales – while highlighting the types of entities likely to be interested, such as private equity firms and strategic buyers through trade sales. This targeted approach ensured our message resonated with their expectations.

One critical point to remember when sharing your Pitch Deck or IM is to ensure that they are only sent to investors with whom you have an existing relationship or have been introduced through a trusted mutual contact. One of the worst outcomes in a fundraising process is having your materials circulated indiscriminately within the investment community. Worse still is when they end up with investors who have explicitly indicated no interest in your sector. If an investor starts receiving your documents from multiple sources, it risks coming across as disorganised – or even desperate.

With everything prepared, the next stage of our journey awaited. We urgently needed further capital before funds ran out, and with my shirts pressed and my shoes polished, I braced myself for the intensity of another investor roadshow.

KEY TAKEAWAYS

- **Cash flow is everything.** And long gone are the days of aggressive technology valuations based purely on top-line growth. Focus on profitability as early as you can and ensure even your early contracts allow you to break even. Loss-leaders are good for no one.
- **Focus on building a diverse revenue stream, across a diverse number of clients.** Over-reliance on one client is dangerous and not viewed positively by the investment community.
- **Shoot for the stars with your investment documentation.** If you proactively anticipate the questions investors will throw at you, you will put less friction between yourself and a large financial commitment from someone.
- **Clarity, confidence and alignment.** Where investment documentation is concerned, I found that these qualities impressed investors: 1) clarity (avoid jargon and make complex ideas easy to understand) 2) confidence (use data, research, and real examples to back up claims – don't just make up unrealistic growth projections) and 3) alignment (investors want to see that the company's vision aligns with current market trends and has the potential for strong returns).

11

THE WHEELS COME OFF

'How Big is Your Brave?'

SARA BAREILLES, MUSICIAN

It was apparent from early in the fundraising process that raising further capital was not going to be an easy task. The appetite of investors for writing cheques to scale-up companies was sadly not what it had once been, and the environment was certainly not helped by the likes of Abraaj Capital going under. Very little international capital was flowing into the Middle East, and on my travels I was repeatedly told that the local investors were spending their time and money shoring up their current exposure to the digital healthcare sector, doubling down on their portfolio companies by providing them with additional capital, rather than investing in new companies.

One of the skills of a venture-capital or private-equity investor is knowing when to double down on one's current portfolio, providing 'follow-on' capital, and when to seek out and invest in new ideas and businesses to diversify one's exposure. Abraaj's demise had not only meant that valuations had fallen, but also that the fundraising cycles in the region were far more protracted. Companies needed to commence their fundraising processes earlier than they had previously, given they would perhaps be under greater scrutiny from a due-diligence perspective.

It was world-renowned investor Warren Buffett who coined the phrase, 'Only when the tide goes out do you learn who has been swimming naked.' This quote is a memorable reminder that success and stability during 'good times' can sometimes be misleading, and only under more challenging conditions do the true weaknesses or vulnerabilities of an individual, business or investment strategy come to light.

Health at Hand had just come through a period of great growth in our user numbers and our client offering, but now that the market was experiencing a downturn it was unclear whether our overall strategy would be exposed. Essentially, we were yet to back up our growth in patient numbers with meaningful revenue figures and were soon to find out if we had prepared well enough during the good times to protect ourselves from the bad. Had we taken on excessive risk? Were we operating unsustainably? Had we really built our technology and operations for scale? Did we have the right team and culture in place to withstand the changing landscape or would we be caught with our pants down, swimming naked?

It was also the time to test our resilience, a key attribute needed by anyone working in the startup and scale-up environment. As a leadership team we needed to display a blend of emotional strength, adaptability and the practical skills to persist, learn and grow through adversity. Resilience allows entrepreneurs to navigate the ups and downs of their journey with greater ease and increase their chances of long-term success. I had long thought of myself as being a highly resilient person, but faced with the challenging environment in which I now found myself, cracks were exposed in my own emotional fortitude and tenacity.

There was a clear moment in the Health at Hand journey where my inability to handle the stress I was subjected to affected me negatively and influenced my behaviour towards my colleagues and my family. This manifested in me being less engaged at home and certainly less patient, but at points I also struggled to explore solutions to my problems in the coherent manner that I had done previously. Faced with a high-pressure situation, essentially the survival of my business, I on occasion struggled to maintain emotional balance and could become distracted more easily. Historically I had seen failures as a learning opportunity rather than a defeat and had proved skilful at extracting valuable lessons in times of adversity. This environment somehow seemed a little different, and I often craved a co-founder or a more engaged board of directors to bounce ideas off.

Perceptions are powerful, and I had to be careful not to seem outwardly panicked. One of the most obvious giveaways of a struggling company is when a founder 'shops' their investment deck far too widely across the investment ecosystem and begins to share their investment material speculatively with people they have never met.

In amongst the panic, I had to keep a cool head and return my focus to the key elements of a successful fundraising process, which I knew only too well. With no obvious investor showing interest from my immediate network, I set about researching the investor landscape again with a desire to target the investors I believed to be a good fit for the company. Most private-equity and venture-capital companies disclose a certain amount of information on their websites, including how much they typically invest, their desired stage of growth and the sectors they are focused on.

Once established, rather than sending unsolicited emails to my target group of investors, I tried to engineer warm introductions to their investment teams through my network. I was also careful to take on board iterative feedback and refine my Pitch Deck as I went along. In an ideal world I would achieve an introduction to the CEO, or at least an executive, within each firm I wanted to approach, in the belief that going in at the top of the organisation would allow me to meet the decision-makers sooner and achieve a 'quick no' which in any sales context is infinitely better than a 'slow no'.

While there were times when I felt my head dropping, there were many more when I still displayed huge self-motivation and discipline. I was increasingly grateful at this time that Sameer was more than good enough to ensure the smooth day-to-day running of the business. In adversity you really see the value of your team, and Sameer, Aftab, Nadim and others were a great source of help and reassurance.

While much of my time was spent attempting to attract capital from the Middle Eastern investor community, mine was a two-pronged approach that also saw me attempt to find a potential trade sale or merger with a more established international telehealth company. This company would most likely not yet be operating in the Middle East but have an interest in buying Health at Hand for both our technology stack and, more importantly, for our Middle Eastern reach and client base.

Valuing a business like Health at Hand was no easy task. While our top-line revenue was still growing from a relatively modest base, our technology stack, customer base and brand really were first class, and in my mind they would all be hugely attractive to potential investors.

In the preceding years, numerous technology companies had raised extraordinary amounts of capital early in their journeys despite having very little revenue, demonstrating the immense confidence investors placed in their innovative business models and growth potential. It was apparent that the landscape was changing, and that the technology bubble was bursting. Uber was one such company always mentioned in conversations about the 2010s tech boom. In 2011, when the ride-hailing platform was still in its infancy, Uber raised $37 million in a Series B funding round. Just two years later, in 2013, its Series C round, led by Google Ventures, secured a staggering $258 million. At this stage, Uber's revenue was still modest, but its aggressive expansion strategy and the scalability of its model allowed it to attract such huge sums.

Similarly, Airbnb achieved remarkable funding success early on. In 2011, it raised $112 million in a Series B round as it began to scale its innovative marketplace connecting travellers with short-term accommodation. The confidence shown by investors was rooted in Airbnb's potential to revolutionise the hospitality sector, even as it faced regulatory and operational hurdles. We all now know how this investment played out, with Airbnb valued today in excess of $70 billion.

Even in the healthcare sector, the likes of Babylon were achieving eye-watering valuations, and Olive, a startup focused on AI-driven automation for hospitals, had recently secured $225.5 million in a late-stage funding round. Though its revenue was relatively low, Olive's promise to reduce inefficiencies in healthcare resonated strongly with investors, who saw vast potential in its scalable solutions.

In most instances I believe there is no science to valuing a business. Numerous models and valuations are often quoted by the investment community, and while they provide a good guide to a company's valuation, and indeed a good tool for comparing different companies in the same sector, the value of a business in my eyes is merely the price someone is willing to pay for it.

Despite my opinion on valuations, I still believed it sensible to report Health at Hand's worth against some common valuation methods, at the very least to provide a guide for potential investors and hopefully to show that there was some method to my madness. It was also not lost on me that valuing the business too high would not only leave me open to scrutiny, but could mean that incoming investors were put off before we'd even had a conversation.

I first offered up a valuation using the Discounted Cash Flow (DCF) method, which involves projecting a company's future cash flows and then discounting them back to the present value using an appropriate discount rate, often the company's weighted average cost of capital (WACC). Essentially, it takes your future growth predictions and determines what these amounts would be worth in today's market. While it accounts for the time-value of money and the long-term potential of a business, it does require accurate forecasting of future cash flows, which are often overstated by entrepreneurs. DCF valuations can also be challenging for early-stage tech companies with limited historical data. And the method can be sensitive to the discount rate used, with small changes in assumptions significantly affecting the outcome. Naturally, founders and investors often find themselves at odds when it comes to determining the discount rate: founders, eager to maximise valuation,

THE WHEELS COME OFF

will typically push for a lower discount, while investors, aiming to minimise their risk and secure greater upside, will advocate for a higher figure. This negotiation becomes a critical balancing act, with both sides working to strike an agreement that reflects both the startup's potential and the investor's appetite for risk.

I also calculated our valuation against what is often called Precedent Transactions, essentially looking at comparable companies to Health at Hand that had raised recently and applying their valuation methodology to our business.

Once you have applied respectable industry methods such as DCF and Precedent Transactions, the hope is that the valuation of your business comes to a number that you are comfortable with.

Back in the UK, Babylon were going from strength to strength, and I had frequently thought of them as a potential acquirer of Health at Hand. Given that I knew Ali, its founder and CEO, reasonably well, to the point of meeting his wife Marie on a few occasions, I determined that they would be a great company for me to approach.

Babylon were growing at a pace that I was hugely envious of, their latest revenue figures of about $323 million a substantial increase on the $79 million they posted the previous year. There was certainly some scepticism from the market that their growth might be overstated and that the AI tool that they were forever showing off to the market might not be quite as advanced as they claimed, but I did have huge respect for Ali and his ambition, and I knew that they had very deep pockets, having raised $550 million in a Series C funding round some eighteen months earlier.

Babylon's business model resonated with me, particularly their focus on increasing growth through their value-based care services and software licensing. They claimed to have already provided around 5.2 million patient consultations and AI interactions globally, demonstrating the scale of their digital-first healthcare platform. These were numbers that we at Health at Hand could only dream of. Babylon were operating in fifteen countries, offering services like the UK National Health Service's 'GP at Hand' and had expanded into markets as diverse as the US and Rwanda. I was aware that they reported a net loss of $76 million for the first half of the year, reflecting the high costs associated with scaling their operations, but this was still fairly commonplace across the digital-healthcare sector.

Fortunately, due to my previous meetings with Ali and some of his senior team, I was able to make sure the Health at Hand investor deck found its way into Ali's inbox, and on the same day his team contacted me to arrange a preliminary investor call. While I didn't necessarily have all the answers to the technical questions posed of me in these meetings, and I'd regularly draft in Aftab and others to support me, I was more than confident that I could handle this initial call myself. Ali determined that his Chief Financial Officer and Head of Sales were best placed for this initial probing and while their questioning was robust, I believe I responded to their queries with authority. Later that day it turned out my initial mission had been accomplished, and Babylon emailed me to set up a more formal two-hour meeting in London the following week.

I decided that rather than travelling alone to London, I'd take Sameer with me for this potentially lifesaving meeting. By this stage, Sameer had a much deeper and more intricate understanding of our product than me. He was also a doctor by profession, and while not as commercial as I was, he was good with people and was someone I trusted to represent the business well.

THE WHEELS COME OFF

As had always been the case with Health at Hand, and rightly so given our financial position, we travelled in economy and both of us found friends to stay with in London as we arrived in good time the day before our meeting. Over the years I had met a number of Babylon's staff at various conferences across the globe and had built up a friendship with one of their commercial directors, Olly, who kindly offered to meet Sameer and I in a café close to Babylon's Sloane Avenue office prior to our meeting.

Olly had always been candid about Babylon's progress, and Sameer and I remain grateful that he was willing to meet us, knowing that we were soon to step into the lion's den. We questioned Olly about the personalities of those we were to meet, inquired about the current and future focus areas for the business, gained useful insights into what made Ali tick personally and professionally and learnt about some of the recent bolt-on acquisitions that Ali and his team had made.

In my view, Sameer and I had two distinct approaches to meeting preparation that reflected the different needs we had in order to feel confident and ready. I have always been someone who values meticulous preparation, ensuring that I am completely familiar with the material well in advance of a meeting. In the hours leading up to the meeting, however, I avoid excessive rechecking or over-analysing, something that served me well in exams at school when I rarely panicked last minute. My best man's speech for my brother's wedding was written a good few weeks in advance, and I only revisited it briefly the night before to refamiliarise myself with its content. This approach allows me to exude a sense of calm assurance in meetings, and from a personal perspective it means I avoid unnecessary stress or mental fatigue. I've also always been pretty good at thinking on my feet; I am good at reacting in the moment and can usually produce a pretty comprehensive response to a question I had not proactively considered beforehand.

In contrast, Sameer's approach was to maintain engagement with the material he was presenting until the very last moment. He found value in continuous refinement and sought to maximise every opportunity to sharpen his insights. In this sense, meeting Olly just before we met Babylon would have been hugely beneficial for Sameer in honing his speech.

Both styles can be hugely effective, and with Sameer the yin to my yang, I believed we were well prepared as we ascended the escalator into Babylon's office.

Having been a salesman for most of my career, I knew the benefit of building rapport in meetings such as this. I had researched Ali's background and was aware that he was born in Rasht, a city in northern Iran, where he spent his early years before fleeing to the UK at the age of sixteen during the turmoil of the Iranian Revolution. Given very few tourists visit Iran, I thought Ali might be impressed to hear that I had been there myself. And to prepare, I reminded myself of the names of some of the famous mosques and monuments I had visited, including the wonderful museum in Tehran celebrating the lives of the Omidvar brothers, who travelled the globe extensively in the 1950s, contributing to anthropology and cultural understanding. Perhaps the opportunity would arise for me to slip my Iranian knowledge into conversation as we travelled in the elevator together. To my mind, there is so much more to a meeting than the presentation you have prepared in advance, and building trust is a crucial step in the process.

Ali had a PhD in engineering physics from University College London and his early career included founding a successful media promotion company, before he went on to work for the likes of

Credit Suisse, Merrill Lynch and Goldman Sachs and then eventually moved into healthcare. As a former banker now entrepreneur myself, with ambitions to level-up the primary-healthcare landscape, maybe my own journey would resonate with him.

Rapport in sales is crucial because it activates fundamental psychological and emotional mechanisms in the brain that foster trust and understanding. When two people connect over shared experiences, interests or values, the brain releases something called oxytocin, often referred to as the 'bonding hormone'. Oxytocin promotes feelings of cooperation, creating a foundation for more meaningful and productive interactions.

This neurochemical response is integral in moving a conversation from transactional to relational, and I was aware that rapport also stimulated the brain's 'mirror neuron system', which enables individuals to empathise by mirroring others' emotions or behaviours. When a salesperson aligns themselves with a client's tone, language or gestures, it creates a subconscious sense of familiarity and comfort. I often use this skill in building presentations or in face-to-face meetings, directly mirroring the language that appears on a company website or that the person opposite you is using. If you use the term 'patients' while they call them 'customers', ensure that you tweak your presentation material so that the word 'customers' is present throughout. This emotional resonance reduces resistance, often making the other party more receptive to your ideas and proposals.

As trust increases in a sales environment, it is often the case that people are more likely to view the salesperson as a partner rather than a persuader, paving the way for collaboration and long-term relationships. It's not the be all and end all – you still need to be selling something of value to the other party – but there is sufficient evidence to suggest that all these skills and tricks do in fact work.

Ali was of a slight build with a bald head, and his looks reminded me of the character Gru from the Minions movie franchise. He had an air of authority about him and a quick mind that could sometimes come across as being a little intimidating.

Sameer and I were shown huge respect by Ali and his team and everyone we met was incredibly complimentary about what we had built, but I couldn't help thinking that our own ambitions paled into insignificance when juxtaposed with their mission and vision. As the meeting progressed, the Babylon team displayed a laser-like focus in drilling into the reasons why we were looking to raise further capital and, equally important, why we had failed to do so thus far. There was no hiding the fact that we only had a few months of runway left. Ali didn't immediately strike me as someone who would be satisfied with merely putting up a bridging loan, and if he liked what he saw, now was his time to strike.

My previous experience of these types of meetings was that they were usually a precursor to a whole raft of additional conversations where you were introduced and further probed by more and more executives from across the business. But this was quite different. Ali made it clear that, while we'd still have to pass Babylon's due-diligence process, which would essentially focus on the strength of our technology stack and our client base, he was prepared to make an offer for Health at Hand there and then. Wow. The great benefit of meeting the boss: a quick decision. Our conversations had moved at speed, and we were about to have a lifeline given to us directly by the CEO of one of the fastest-growing digital healthcare businesses in the world.

THE WHEELS COME OFF

When Ali's offer arrived, I don't know why I was so surprised by how aggressive it was. He was after all an ex-investment banker sitting opposite an entrepreneur who had few other options and a limited amount of time to find a solution.

Ali was effectively suggesting a share swap – a business acquisition where no cash changes hands. Babylon were offering their own shares in exchange for full ownership of Health at Hand. This is a common practice in mergers and acquisitions, particularly when the buyer wants to preserve cash, or the seller believes in the growth potential of the buyer's stock, and I had worked on numerous transactions like this in my own banking career.

The challenge here was that Ali didn't need to preserve cash. He just didn't value Health at Hand highly enough to offer a cash-plus-equity or a pure-cash investment option. And furthermore, the equity he was offering in Babylon, in exchange for the full acquisition of Health at Hand, valued the business at less than half what we were seeking. I did, however, understand his logic. Whereas a traditional healthcare acquirer might want us for our technology stack as opposed to our client base, Babylon's technology platform was far superior to ours, and he effectively only wanted us for our Middle Eastern foothold and our clients.

Receiving an offer to buy your company can evoke a mix of conflicting emotions. On the one hand, there was a sense of validation and excitement: Ali Parsa was still willing to invest significantly in Health at Hand and it was a sign that my hard work had paid off, that my efforts had resonated with leaders in the sector. However, with such aggressive terms, I felt discomfited and hesitant. I don't blame Ali. He saw me walk into his office and was quick enough to determine that we were on our knees and in a weak negotiating position, but I left the Babylon office torn between a) my admiration for Ali and the pull of a future for Health at Hand with Babylon and b) the fear of being rushed into a decision and a full sale of the business for a price that I didn't think necessarily represented fair value.

Sameer and I returned to the Middle East, thanking Ali for his kind offer and letting him know that we would come back to him within a matter of weeks. He made it clear that this was his one and only offer, and that there was no room for negotiating either the price or the structure of the deal.

Our London trip had not been fruitless. We had an offer, albeit not one at a level we had previously considered. While it would give Health at Hand the lifeline we were seeking, we pondered whether it was the right thing to do, whether or not it received the approval of the Health at Hand board, who were required to sign off on any sale of the business. Perhaps first I could use his offer to generate some competitive pressure with other potential suitors.

Back in Dubai there was some nervousness amongst the staff. As a CEO, leading a workforce through uncertain times requires not just strategic decision-making but also a deep sense of care and empathy for the individuals who make up the team. My priority was to foster a sense of security, even in challenging moments such as this, by maintaining open and honest communication. But it was becoming harder to put a positive spin on our situation given that I knew our cash flow was running down quickly. I have always believed that transparency builds trust, so I made a point to share a full update about the company's situation on my return, making it clear to the staff that we were in a relatively precarious position and discussing the offer that we had on the table from Babylon. I was conscious of the stress and unease that this would inevitably cause members of the team, but even if the news wasn't ideal, I was hopeful that some clarity would ultimately reduce the anxiety in the long run and help everyone feel more connected to the process.

I knew my staff well and had put considerable care into my relationships with them. The majority of the team were either the main breadwinners in their household, or at the very least their salaries were absolutely required to support their lifestyles, contributing to their rent, their food or their children's education.

Stress and uncertainty can take a significant toll, and I have already alluded to the stress I myself felt at times during this period. I strived to encourage a culture where people could speak openly about their concerns and decided to host regular question-and-answer sessions in the office where nothing was off limits. I aimed to show that I cared about every individual's emotional health, and the reality was that I absolutely did. I introduced some small and simple gestures, like allowing flexibility in terms of working hours and allowing people to spend as much time as they wanted working away from the office.

I was also determined to maintain a sense of purpose and belonging within the workforce. In difficult times, it's easy to feel disconnected or uncertain about one's role. While I didn't want to sugar-coat the position we were in, I made it a priority to remind everyone of the larger mission we were working towards, and I made it clear that the journey was not over yet and that I'd keep fighting each and every day for my team. The great thing about us working in healthcare was that there were regular stories about how we were helping patients via our product, and each week I posted such tales on our company portal.

We continued to celebrate even the small wins that brought us closer to our goal, and I made even more of an effort to recognise individual staff and team contributions, both publicly and personally, reinforcing the belief that each person was vital to Health at Hand's resilience and our future. Showing that the senior management and I were invested in individual growth, no matter the external challenges we were facing, hopefully demonstrated that our commitment to our brilliant and dedicated team was more than mere words. I was hopeful that my efforts would remind the workforce that they were valued and that we were navigating these challenges together.

In adversity you really see the value of your staff, and I was lucky to have a brilliantly supportive team who I believed were 100 per cent convinced that the leadership and I were doing everything possible to help our predicament.

We still had some options. I hadn't given up on raising further capital from the venture-capital and private-equity ecosystem, where I was well connected. But I also looked at more strategic routes to funding. Our clients were likely to not want to see us fail, and there were a number of private clinic and hospital groups in the region who were likely to benefit personally from our product. Then, of course, there was Nextcare, our biggest client by some distance, who had publicly stated their desire to roll out Health at Hand's service even further and wider across their client base.

I was also fortunate that, through a connection from one of my board members, I met an investment group, Latham X, in Dubai who also had an interest in what we were doing. They did, however, have question marks over our revenue numbers, and they ordinarily invested into growth-stage companies, those a little more advanced in their journey than Health at Hand.

THE WHEELS COME OFF

After what seemed like tens of meetings in the various coffee shops, restaurants and members clubs of the Dubai International Finance Centre, Latham X were persuaded to sign a term sheet to the tune of $4 million. On the surface this represented a huge win and would bring much more than bridging capital; it could, in fact, extend our runway for a further thirty to thirty-six months and might potentially be the silver bullet we needed.

A term sheet is a non-binding document that outlines the key terms and conditions of a proposed business agreement. Typically, it serves as a preliminary agreement to ensure all parties are aligned on the main investment points before a deal moves into the more detailed phase of due diligence and finally the legally binding phase of drafting final contracts, like shareholder agreements.

While this was undoubtedly a positive step forward, I remained acutely aware that the document in question from Latham X was not legally binding, and I was left with a lingering concern in my gut about Latham X's true intentions. I couldn't shake the possibility that they viewed the term sheet less as a definitive commitment and more a strategic gesture. In my mind, their existing relationship with one of my board members suggested that they might be willing to sign the term sheet purely to help us attract interest from other investors. Once sufficient momentum had been generated, they could potentially withdraw from the process without committing further, leaving us back at square one. This added an additional layer of complexity to an already precarious situation.

In a final, decisive effort to turn the tide, I went back to where it all began. I scheduled a meeting with Christian at Nextcare's head office on Sheikh Zayed Road. Up to this point, in our conversations I had carefully avoided any mention of our fragile financial position. However, I decided it was time to approach the situation with complete transparency. I believed that honesty would strengthen the trust between us.

I laid out the reality: unless we secured fresh capital or identified a buyer within the next six months, our business would inevitably fall over. I posed the critical question: would Nextcare or their parent company Allianz, having already rolled out the Health at Hand platform to a significant percentage of their regional customers, really want to see us fail?

Christian, as I've previously noted, was an astute and highly strategic operator. His response reflected both his commercial acumen and his understanding of the gravity of our situation. He told me that he wasn't particularly surprised by what I had revealed. He would know better than anyone given the advantageous commercial terms he had previously negotiated with me. He expressed his conviction that Health at Hand deserved to command a long-term place within Nextcare's portfolio of products and that he loved working with our team and saw the value of our partnership.

Christian wanted to acquire Health at Hand, notwithstanding the fact that any decision would require approval from his paymasters at Allianz in Germany. His enthusiasm to make something happen was reassuring, but the matter was now in the hands of his senior decision-makers.

With that, we entered a waiting game. To facilitate Allianz's decision-making process, I furnished Christian with a comprehensive data room, containing every conceivable detail about our business. The next steps would be out of our hands, and the days ahead would test our patience and resilience as we awaited their response. It was a pivotal moment, and one that would determine the future not just of the company, but of everyone who had dedicated themselves to its success.

KEY TAKEAWAYS

- **Resilience is a crucial skill in business.** If you can navigate challenges and adapt to changes, you have a better chance of sustaining growth over the long term. In today's unpredictable economic and global landscape, resilience serves as the foundation for enduring success.
- **Plan early for an equity raise.** Particularly when the market conditions are not favourable. While our own fundraising process had already been ongoing for a few months, I could possibly have started the process earlier, or at the very least prioritised building my network of venture-capital and private-equity investors while the going was good.
- **Make sure the value that you place on your business is well thought out.** If you go in too high, it will be off-putting to incoming investors, and I guarantee you'll be asked to justify the number you have come up with.
- **Hustle, hustle and hustle some more.** And never give up – it's not over until it's over.

12

LIMPING OVER THE LINE

'Success is not final; failure is not fatal: it is
the courage to continue that counts'

WINSTON CHURCHILL

When Allianz's offer to buy the business finally came through, it represented the most favourable option for Health at Hand. Unfortunately, in the preceding weeks, I had failed to pull a rabbit out of the proverbial hat and the only firm interest we had was from Babylon, Allianz and Latham X, who, just as I had predicted, had decided that the opportunity was 'not quite right for them'.

The options I had on the table from Babylon and Allianz were markedly different in terms of how they were structured, and I had to carefully consider which provided the best outcome for my shareholders. The frequency of my contact with the board of directors increased significantly as we bashed through the terms of the offers and options before us.

When compared to Babylon's offer, the Allianz proposition seemingly ticked more boxes. Allianz had attributed a greater valuation to the business, and while their valuation fell short of what I had previously thought we might be worth, being a full cash offer it represented an opportunity to immediately return capital to my shareholders – rather than swapping Health at Hand shares for those in Babylon Health Limited.

When selling a business, choosing between a cash offer and an equity swap offer is a critical decision, each coming with its own set of advantages and risks. A cash offer often stands out as the more straightforward and secure option, providing several key benefits and of course guarantees immediate liquidity. Money today is always considered better than money tomorrow, and in our case this was true not least because of the uncertainty that the Babylon offer came with – including the possible default or poor performance of the Babylon business further down the line.

In our case, Allianz's offer enabled Health at Hand and our shareholders to realise the value of the offer up front, without the need to wait for a payout at a future date. For sellers seeking certainty and control, two things myself and the board had all decided were priorities, the predictability of Allianz's cash offer was more appealing.

Additionally, a cash offer eliminates the complexity and the ongoing commitment associated with holding equity in another company. With an equity swap, the seller becomes a shareholder in the acquiring business, which may require involvement in decision-making, navigating integration challenges or having to stomach potential dilution of ownership over time. In my case it would almost certainly have required me to commit to at least twenty-four months as a Babylon employee. A cash transaction would allow us all sever ties cleanly, avoiding any future entanglements with Allianz and Health at Hand's future performance.

To my mind, Allianz's offer represented my mid-case scenario – it was nowhere near as good as taking a multi-million-dollar investment from a strategic investor in return for a minority stake in the business, which would have allowed me to keep the Health at Hand dream alive, but far better than our cashflow gently dribbling away and having to close down the business.

Emotionally I was feeling particularly drained from the challenge of securing this investment. It had been a long and protracted process, and aside from the hundreds of investment meetings I had attended, I had also conducted regular calls with my board, my shareholders and my staff as I sought to keep everyone abreast of the developments. Truth be told, my love for the business had also been severely tested in the previous few months, and I was happy to bring the investment raise to a conclusion.

I was particularly pleased that Allianz's offer would allow me the opportunity to make good on my promise from Day One with regards to staff ownership. The majority of the team had equity options, which had vested, and as these individuals officially appeared on our capitalisation table, they would be receiving a cheque.

Allianz and Health at Hand signed a term sheet outlining the headline terms of the acquisition. With the reassurances Allianz had given me and the fact I had a longstanding professional relationship with Christian, I was confident that we would see this transaction through to its conclusion. I was also comforted by the fact that within the term sheet there was a specific target execution date, which was twelve weeks after its signing.

With only two months of cash flow left in the business, I needed some additional reassurances from Christian. I needed Allianz to confirm that they would take care of our monthly cash flow until the transaction had been concluded, even if it had to be delayed beyond the twelve-week target, and that they would transfer working capital each month into the business, without it affecting the valuation. Christian willingly obliged. This de-risked the transaction a little for Health at Hand and meant that I could feel relatively relaxed if the close date ran over the predicted target date.

I also wanted some reassurance around my staff. I didn't want Allianz just acquiring our technology IP, our clients and our brand – I wanted to ensure that the full Health at Hand team would form part of the transaction. This was incredibly important to me, given the loyalty they had all shown me.

As part of the transaction process, I was required to provide a personal data file for every member of the team. This included sensitive personal details such as addresses, identification documents, college certificates, resumes, current salaries and pension liabilities. In the UAE, employees accumulate an end-of-service benefit, akin to a pension, based on their base salary and their years of service. This liability is ultimately borne by their employer, who must pay the amount in full when an employee leaves their employment. To streamline the process, I prepared a detailed spreadsheet outlining each employee's current salary and their end-of-service entitlement, which I shared with Christian.

Christian, known for his hard-nosed negotiation style, responded promptly with a revised spreadsheet. Next to each employee's name, he had inserted 'proposed new salary' figures, slashing future salaries for many of the staff by between twenty and thirty per cent. Moreover, Allianz's initial bargaining position was that all pension liabilities would be paid from the sales proceeds rather than by Allianz themselves.

These two areas of salary reductions and pension liabilities were red lines for me. I made it unequivocally clear that I would not entertain Allianz's offer to acquire the business unless all employees were guaranteed their current salaries and that their pension entitlements were honoured by Allianz. They were not only exceptional professionals but also critical to the company's success, and I knew they were vital to the future of the business. Their expertise and dedication would be invaluable assets to Allianz and Nextcare going forward, and without them, the business's value and its ability to deliver on its ambition would be significantly diminished.

With regards the pension liabilities, I directed Christian's attention to a number of recent company-acquisition transactions in the UAE where the buyer had taken on the end of service liabilities in full. Given that Babylon's offer was still on the table, I leveraged this as a bargaining tool, emphasising that I was prepared to walk away from the negotiating table if necessary. I don't believe Christian was ever being unreasonable or unkind. He was a commercial guy just trying to protect the best interests of his own employer, and perhaps only a mouthpiece for Allianz's desired position rather than this being his own personal stance. But I was keen to negotiate a much better outcome for the team. While the stance was risky, it was one I felt strongly about.

Allianz were (and still are) a Fortune 500 company, meaning that they were one of the 500 largest companies in the world by gross income. While I appreciated that they would need to conduct considerable due diligence on Health at Hand before the transaction was concluded, it was inconceivable to me that the transaction would take many months more than they had originally predicted. Over the course of my career, I had been involved in numerous merger-and-acquisition transactions with companies of a similar size to Health at Hand and Allianz, but I was still surprised that, for a company with Health at Hand's relatively lean operation and short trading history, the transaction seemed to drag and drag. Given that the acquisition was less than Allianz's average $50 million transaction size, it seemed to me that we weren't top of their list of priorities.

Conducting due diligence on a fledgeling technology business is meant to be easy, but nothing's easy if every paperclip is scrutinised and your acquirer seemingly has a 'Director of Post-It-Notes'. The level of detail that Allianz went into prior to concluding the transaction was perhaps reassuring, but I still found it staggering at times. As you might expect, I personally took on the role as the lead transaction-negotiator for Health at Hand, and it proved to be an incredibly time-consuming process as I fought to respond to such frequent and detailed information requests from their German head office in a timely manner.

Over the following months, I grappled with the escalating uncertainty surrounding the transaction. The acquisition moved at Allianz's pace, with them seemingly oblivious to the strain such delays placed on my team.

During the process, I made a deliberate effort to retain enough funds in Health at Hand's bank account to cover the costs of closing our own operating entities once the acquisition had concluded, as well as maintaining a small buffer of cash for any final liabilities we might have, such as outstanding transactional legal fees. Beyond that, however, we did indeed run out of money two months into the transaction. On the penultimate day of each subsequent month, I would nervously send across our working capital requirements to Abdullah, Nextcare's Chief Financial Officer, and face an anxious wait for the funds to arrive in our bank account before initiating our payroll. Frequently the funds would arrive late, something myself and the team were not accustomed to.

I vividly recall one surreal weekend when I was lying on my bed in a hotel in Sri Lanka, hours before attending Sameer's wedding, trying to persuade Abdullah to wire the now ten-days-overdue funds so I could pay my team. It was a stressful and bizarre juxtaposition of responsibilities. Abdullah himself was a wonderfully charming and professional person to conduct business with, and I put the payment delays down to the small size of the Health at Hand acquisition, as I have mentioned previously, and perhaps some communication challenges between Allianz in Germany and their Middle Eastern subsidiary.

On multiple occasions I became the target for frustration from employees struggling to cope with receiving their salaries late. While it would have been easy to place the blame squarely on Allianz, I appreciated they were only doing their job, and I chose to shoulder the responsibility myself. I fronted up to my team, absorbing their frustration and addressing their concerns directly. I had immense empathy for what they were going through, knowing how unsettling it was for them, and my priority remained preserving morale and doing everything in my power to ensure the eventual success of the transaction.

On at least one occasion, the monthly working capital was not only late, but it did not represent the full amount, meaning I had to hold back some monthly salaries and would only be able to pay staff what we had received. Depending on the month, this might amount to 60 or 70 per cent of their usual salaries on a pro rata basis. This situation was far from ideal.

While I completely understood the angst of the staff, unbeknown to them, during this period I always ensured that I was paid last, persuaded by the book *Leaders Eat Last: Why Some Teams Pull Together and Others Don't* by Simon Sinek. This book explores the dynamics of leadership and teamwork, emphasising the role of empathy, trust and sacrifice in fostering successful organisations. Drawing on examples from the military, corporate environments and social psychology, Sinek argues that great leaders prioritise the well-being of their teams, creating environments of safety where collaboration and innovation thrive. Far from claiming to be a 'great' leader myself, I was persuaded to do what I did by Sinek's notion of the 'Circle of Safety', where leaders shield their teams from external pressures, enabling them to focus on shared goals.

The delay in finalising the transaction, though stressful, proved to have unexpected advantages, providing me with additional time to negotiate with Christian. During this period, I successfully persuaded him that the entire Health at Hand team would be included as part of the acquisition. I secured commitments that their full salaries would be maintained upon their transition to Nextcare, and that Allianz would fully cover their pensions. Standing firm in these negotiations paid off, delivering a much-needed boost of positive news for the team.

Some members of the team had been understandably anxious about their future, particularly with the prospect of becoming part of a much larger organisation. The shift from being integral players in a dynamic, flexible technology startup to joining a more structured corporate environment would no doubt take significant adjustment. However, the reassurance regarding their roles and benefits helped to alleviate concerns and reaffirm their importance within the company's broader vision.

Once I had negotiated the team's future, the attention turned towards me. 'And what about you, Charlie?' Christian asked. 'There is huge key-person risk here. You are the face of the business in the region and an extremely high-profile thought-leader in the sector.' Ironically, I had just been awarded the MENA Telehealth CEO of the Year for the third year in a row and was at the time on the front cover of *CEO Monthly* magazine. It was hard to escape the fact that I was synonymous with the brand.

In all honesty, I was drained and ready to move on. I'd given my all to Health at Hand, and as other entrepreneurs can attest, you never really have evenings or weekends to yourself. I had loved the majority of the journey, but with my family in the UK and with little interest in witnessing my 'baby' being consumed by a large German insurance conglomerate in Allianz, I was keen to step aside as quickly as I could.

I believe Christian was aware of this, and while I did remain involved for a few more months to ensure a soft landing following the conclusion of the acquisition, both he and I were more than convinced that Sameer could take on my role and push Health at Hand to greater heights.

So, with the contract signed and the money* on its way into Health at Hand's bank account, it was over.

In Ernest Hemingway's novel *The Sun Also Rises*, a character named Mike is asked how he went bankrupt. 'Two ways,' he answers. 'Gradually, then suddenly.' Ultimately, Health at Hand's end came in much the same way. Gradually, and then suddenly. One day we were fine and the next we were not.

While Health at Hand didn't go bankrupt, far from it in fact, it did on occasion feel to me like someone had died. I'd poured my

---

* The actual amount is subject to a confidentiality agreement.

heart and soul into the business over a period of four years, and there was no one else on the planet who would feel the pain I felt at its loss. Some staff and shareholders no doubt felt let down, particularly because we all had such ambition for Health at Hand, but I myself felt that I had personally failed.

Selling your own business is a deeply emotional process for a founder. It represents the culmination of years of hard work, sacrifice and dedication, and in my case a journey filled with mixed emotions, ranging from pride and excitement to grief and uncertainty.

One of the strongest positive emotions is a sense of achievement. For many founders, selling their business signifies a validation of their vision, effort and the impact they have created. A successful sale can feel like reaching the pinnacle of entrepreneurial success, particularly if the buyer is a company or individual that the founder admires. This excitement is often coupled with a sense of financial security, as the proceeds from the sale may enable the founder to achieve personal goals, provide for their family or fund new ventures. However, I didn't feel like this at all. Any money I would personally receive was life-enhancing rather than life-changing, and my overriding feeling was that I had let a lot of people down, particularly those who had invested substantial amounts of money into the business and were hopeful of huge returns.

A decision to sell is rarely without its emotional challenges. For many founders, their business is deeply personal, often feeling like an extension of their identity. Letting go can create a profound sense of loss as the founder relinquishes control over something they've built from the ground up. Questions about how the new owners will treat the business, employees and customers can weigh heavily, especially if the founder feels a strong sense of responsibility to their team and stakeholders.

The sale process itself can also be emotionally taxing. Negotiations may bring moments of doubt, frustration and even conflict, as founders balance securing favourable terms with giving up control. If the decision is driven by financial necessity or external pressures, it can often bring feelings of failure or regret, and this was absolutely the case with Health at Hand, even if the sale ultimately benefited the business.

Despite feelings of disappointment, there was also a mild sense of relief. Running a business often involves relentless stress, and a sale can offer the founder a chance to step back, recharge and pursue other passions. The relief for me was tinged with anxiety about 'what's next', and I was and still am aware of many founders who struggle with the issue of purpose after stepping away from their entrepreneurial identity.

In short, selling a business is an emotional rollercoaster, blending pride, joy and relief with uncertainty, loss and introspection. While the financial rewards and sense of accomplishment can often be significant, the emotional cost of letting go of a deeply personal creation is equally profound. For founders, finding balance, processing their feelings and planning for the future are crucial steps in navigating this complex experience.

In my case, there was no 'champagne moment' when the sale proceeds hit the company account, and I had had little time to focus on my own future. I'd not fully delivered on the mission, vision and values that Amy, Aftab, Jenna and I had set out four years earlier as we explored what Health at Hand could achieve. I also acknowledge and apologise for the fact that as a business we did not achieve the financial returns that a number of my shareholders were hopeful of. I do, however, know in my heart that this wasn't due to any lack of effort on my part or that of my team.

*

Reflecting on Health at Hand today, and the experience it gave me, I cannot help but think of the deep regret I would carry now if I hadn't taken the leap and started my own business. Even though we failed to achieve unicorn status, the journey itself was invaluable and the thought of not experiencing it at all is far more painful than the lessons I learnt from the outcome. All those who invested into Health at Hand were experienced investors and were aware that there was huge risk in backing a first-time entrepreneur in a new subsector of healthcare. To achieve unicorn status would have put us in a very small minority of successful technology businesses.

Had I stayed in my comfort zone, I would have avoided the risk, but I would have also missed out on the growth. I would have wondered, 'What could I have achieved if I had tried?' That lingering question would have followed me, casting a shadow over everything I did. The fear of failure might have felt daunting then, but now I realise that never trying would have been the true failure.

Health at Hand taught me more than I ever could have learned in a classroom or a nine-to-five job. It showed me the true values of persistence, discipline and problem-solving. These have enriched my personal and working life, and with the often-used phrase 'you learn more in adversity' in mind, I believe there are lessons for us all in these pages, be you a current or aspiring entrepreneur, or simply someone looking to improve in areas of their business life.

If I hadn't started Health at Hand, I would have missed the opportunity to discover my own potential. There is a satisfaction in creating something from scratch, and often those bashing you from the sidelines have never been bold enough to embark on their own journey and test themselves in the same manner. It's not just the end result; it's the courage to begin.

Regret comes not only from missed opportunities, but from a lack of stories that define who we are. Starting my own business added a chapter to my life that I'll always be proud of, no matter the outcome. I met people, built relationships, made friendships and gained insights that have shaped me. And I am proud of the way myself and the team built the business, behaving with integrity and professionalism at all times.

For the most part I feel incredibly lucky for having the opportunity to pursue my dream. Sure, there were sleepless nights and moments of self-doubt, but there was also a thrill in making decisions, strategising and seeing ideas come to life. Without the experience of entrepreneurship, I would have missed the chance to challenge myself in ways I never thought possible.

Most importantly, starting my own business redefined my relationship with success. If I hadn't tried, I might still believe that success is only about hitting milestones or amassing financial gain. Now I understand it's about growth, resilience and the lessons learned along the way. The experience challenged me and changed me, and I wouldn't trade that for anything.

In their heart of hearts, I hope my team, my board and my shareholders know that I left everything out there and did all in my power to make Health at Hand a success.

And the fact I was brave enough to take my first steps is on its own a huge accomplishment.

No regrets. I dared to dream of unicorns.

KEY TAKEAWAYS

- **Look after your bottom line.** While I've mentioned this point before, it's worth labouring: long gone are the heady days of large investments finding their way into unprofitable technology businesses. Your business model must prove that you can at least break even and stand on your own two feet before too long.
- **The structure of your exit transaction is crucial.** In Health at Hand's case, the cash offer from Allianz guaranteed immediate liquidity and allowed us to realise the value of the acquisition upfront. This was a significant reason why we chose this exit route, and it was fortunate that we did so. Babylon had their own problems a few years later and their downfall was swift and severe. Had we chosen to pursue this exit route, Health at Hand shareholders would have been returned less than £1 for every £100 invested.
- **Fight hard.** I still take great pride in the fact I fought for my staff's salaries and pensions to be paid by Allianz. The protracted acquisition afforded me a few more weeks to successfully negotiate these points.
- **You don't always get that champagne moment.** When the money hit our account, my overriding emotions were of disappointment and regret. The transaction had dragged on for a number of months, and the outcome was not what I had once imagined. Be prepared. The euphoria of a business sale often differs from expectations, especially in today's digital landscape where social media bombards us with success stories that rarely depict reality.

13

CONCLUSION

'I knew that if I failed, I wouldn't regret that, but I knew the one thing I might regret is not trying'

JEFF BEZOS

The truth of the matter is that 99 per cent of people shouldn't start their own business. You won't work fewer hours, in fact you'll probably work twice as hard as you ever have, and you'll be married to your phone during weekends and holidays.

You won't do 'more of what you love', you'll do human resources and finances and administrative tasks and contracts and business development and sales.

You probably won't earn more, given it's not a good look for founders to pay themselves too much.

But for the 1 per cent of us, starting our own business is a necessary step in our journey. I, for one, would never have been totally satisfied until I'd given it a go.

But be warned: most businesses fail. Receiving a regular salary and the additional benefits associated with being employed, such as a pension and free healthcare, is a much safer option.

I wouldn't change my experience with Health at Hand for the world, despite the stress and the challenges I faced in the latter months while at the helm of the business.

As Tony Robbins, the well-known motivational speaker and personal-development coach observed, 'Success leaves clues.' But so does failure.

Here are some tips that just might help and inspire any current or aspirational entrepreneurs, learnt both in times of success and of adversity:

Be Lucky

I have a theory about luck – you make your own! Don't complain that 'now is not the right time' or that you'd have loved to move abroad, but you 'never received an offer' to do so. Guess what – neither did I. I made it happen because I wanted it to happen, and I realised that graft and tenacity were required to realise my dreams. Ultimately, getting on a plane to Hong Kong with Claire was one of the best decisions of my life.

Don't blame others or bemoan your own lack of luck. Make your own luck by working hard and being street-smart. Network hard, be a sponge of information, return favours and be kind to people. Rarely does the perfect job just land in your lap. Get out there and opportunities will come your way.

CONCLUSION

Make Mistakes – but Only the Same Mistake Once

Take risks. Be bold. Build quickly. And 'move fast and break things'. Losing is simply learning. But you need to have the appetite to learn quickly when you make mistakes. Be self-critical and be honest. And remember that if you aren't making mistakes, you might not be pushing as hard as you should be.

Listen and Respond to Market Feedback

Entrepreneurs need to have their eyes and ears open and must be adaptable. Actively seeking feedback is a great skill and often serves to highlight areas for improvement, necessary features, or even shifts in market demand that the entrepreneur had not anticipated.

By continually iterating on your product based on real user insights, you will better align your offering with market needs, ultimately driving customer satisfaction and growth.

This continual iteration will lead to a more refined product and, consequently, a stronger position when approaching potential investors or buyers.

Stay open to constructive criticism, and prioritising customer feedback. It will foster a culture of innovation that can set the stage for future success.

Get Your Idea Out There – Quickly

I've seen too many companies spend months and even years hypothesising over their idea and building endless prototypes and MVPs in a darkened room. Advice from your co-founders, your friends and your mum will likely be biased.

Get your idea in front of your potential buyers as soon you can. It may sound brave, and you may feel exposed, but I guarantee that it's the quickest way to learn. You won't know how much work you still have to do until your potential buyers provide feedback.

Forget Doing an MBA – this Is Your MBA

The traditional education system doesn't fully prepare you for entrepreneurship. For a thought-provoking perspective, watch Sir Ken Robinson's TED Talk 'Do Schools Kill Creativity?' It's a witty yet critical take on how formal education often stifles original thinking.

My mother once told me, 'You only really learn to drive once you have passed your test and you are out there on the road alone,' and it's the same with the business world. Real experience, not endless qualifications, is what truly equips you for success.

Focus on Plan A

When starting a business, it's essential to commit fully to your vision and resist distractions. Craft a clear, actionable plan and stay loyal to it, even when the going gets tough. While there may be moments when adjusting course is necessary, these pivots should be thought through and aligned with your core mission, rather than reactions to every minor challenge.

Believe in your original idea and its potential impact – this confidence will provide the strength to persevere through early obstacles and will keep you on a steady path towards achieving your ultimate goal.

CONCLUSION

Ruthless Prioritisation

Entrepreneurs often feel the pull to explore every idea and tackle every opportunity, but the truth is that attempting to do too much can dilute your efforts. Prioritisation isn't just a strategy, it's a discipline that involves saying 'no' more than 'yes'.

Focus on developing a 'hero product' – a single offering that truly captures the essence of your brand and meets a significant need in the market. Dedicate yourself to making this product outstanding rather than spreading yourself thin across multiple ventures. By committing to doing one thing exceptionally well, you establish a foundation that can support future growth, without losing your identity.

Don't Micro-Manage

One of the most crucial skills for a leader is the ability to trust their team. Hire talented, passionate people, and then give them the autonomy to show their strengths. Offer clear guidance, communicate expectations and provide support, but avoid the urge to control every detail of their work.

Micro-managing stifles creativity, creates frustration and signals a lack of confidence in your team members. If you feel the need to oversee every small action, it may indicate that you haven't yet built a team you trust.

Strong leadership is about empowering others to deliver their best and then recognising and rewarding their efforts.

Ruffle Some Feathers

Disruption is at the heart of any impactful business. To make a difference you must be willing to challenge existing norms and push back against established players. This doesn't mean antagonising people unnecessarily, but playing it safe is unlikely to cut it.

By ruffling a few feathers, you force people to take notice. Position yourself as a forward-thinking leader and seek to carve out a unique place in the market.

Always Speak Well of the Competition

One of the most powerful ways to establish credibility is by focusing on what sets you apart, without disparaging others. Highlight the unique value your solution brings rather than the weaknesses of rival products.

Be gracious, collaborative and open to sharing best practices, even with competitors – this approach not only builds goodwill but also fosters a culture of mutual respect within the industry and reflects confidence in your own offering.

Enjoy the Ride

The journey of entrepreneurship is full of challenges, but it's also full of moments worth savouring. Take time to appreciate both the wins and the learning experiences, no matter how small. Don't get bogged down by every minor setback; keep your focus on the bigger picture and remember why you started in the first place.

Developing this perspective will not only make the journey more enjoyable but will also keep you energised and motivated.

CONCLUSION

Entrepreneurship isn't just about the destination – it's about embracing every stage of the process, about growing as a person and about finding fulfilment along the way.

Teach Yourself Emotional Resilience

Success in business, as in life, often hinges on emotional resilience. Cultivate the ability to handle both triumphs and failures with a balanced mindset. Celebrate your successes, but don't let them define you, and learn from setbacks without internalising them.

This level-headed approach will allow you to navigate the ups and downs of entrepreneurship with composure and clarity. Emotional resilience doesn't mean suppressing emotions; it's about maintaining perspective. This mindset is a critical asset, allowing you to stay focused, adapt to challenges and continue pushing forward without being swayed by temporary highs or lows.

Get a Mentor

As the sole founder of Health at Hand, I often faced moments of isolation and found myself making decisions without anyone to consult or any prior experience to rely on. While these challenges ultimately taught me valuable lessons, having a mentor could have made a huge and positive difference.

A mentor may have provided me with guidance, challenged my thinking, offered encouragement and helped me navigate difficult times. To me, a mentor isn't necessarily someone from your team or even your advisory board. Instead, it's someone who understands your business but maintains enough distance to offer objective, caring and honest advice. An independent mentor can be an invaluable resource, offering insights and support from a fresh perspective.

Think Different

Apple's 'Think Different' slogan, introduced in 1997, was a rallying cry that celebrated creativity, individuality and innovation. It's difficult to imagine, but at the time Apple was on its knees.

'Think Different' positioned Apple as a brand for those who see the world differently, challenging the status quo and rethinking traditional approaches. It was more than just a slogan. It was a call to action and a redefinition of the company's identity, with figures like Albert Einstein, Mahatma Gandhi and Martin Luther King Jr featured in the advertising campaign.

The slogan had a dual purpose. For consumers it conveyed that Apple was a brand with progressive values. For Apple's internal culture it reinforced Apple's mission to innovate fearlessly, inspiring employees to take risks and think beyond conventional boundaries.

That one phrase cleverly summed up exactly what Apple were about. You don't have to be richer, brighter or better educated than the other guy or girl. But you do have to 'think different' to analyse a real problem and find and build a viable solution.

When I incubated Health at Hand, the concept was highly ambitious for its time, and the technical and regulatory challenges we faced often seemed insurmountable. Imagine trying to build a business around real-time video communication in a country where VoIP is flat-out banned. Imaging trying to launch a telehealth solution in a country where there was no regulation to operate such a business. Imagine trying to change consumer behaviours in a sector as sacrosanct as healthcare, persuading patients that the clinical outcomes from seeing a doctor remotely were the same as when seeing a doctor face to face.

But Health at Hand wasn't just a story about overcoming regulatory roadblocks – it was about pushing boundaries when the odds seem stacked against us. In this sense I really was a true pioneer in the digital healthcare space as one of the first entrepreneurs globally to build a digital-healthcare solution focused on the underserved populations of the emerging markets.

So, what valuable lessons did Health at Hand teach me throughout my experience?

Lesson 1: Technology Is the Enabler, Not the Hero

In digital healthcare, especially telemedicine, technology is just a vehicle to deliver what really matters, namely improved access and reduced costs. We had to not only engineer solutions for seamless video calls, but also ensure that we kept on the right side of the UAE's regulatory environment.

My key takeaway here is don't get too attached to the technology; instead focus on solving the real pain point. In our case, this was delivering timely medical consultations that met the regulatory requirements, at a low price point.

This lesson extends beyond the emerging markets in which we operated. Whether you're innovating in digital health or other sectors, your goal should be to anticipate future challenges and adapt accordingly. With advancements like 5G, cloud computing and AI, the technological barriers are falling – but regulatory and consumer acceptance remain hurdles.

Future unicorns in the digital healthcare sector will not only leverage cutting-edge tools like AI-driven diagnostics, but will also navigate complex regulations by focusing on patient-centred design. The patient must be at the heart of the solution.

Lesson 2: Navigating Regulation Is Half the Battle

Even when we overcame the technical challenges, regulation was always looming. This is where startups often falter. Technology founders can often engineer breakthrough products, but without understanding the regulatory landscape, those innovations may not see the light of day.

Understand the rules of the game. If the rules are too restrictive, find ways to innovate within them. In the UAE, we focused on clinical guidelines, patient safety and regulatory compliance from day one and knew that without regulatory support we wouldn't have a chance.

Future unicorn-builders in health tech should pay attention to policy trends like data privacy (e.g., GDPR, HIPAA), AI regulations and telehealth reimbursement models. The winners will be those who engage regulators early and help shape the rules, not just follow them.

Lesson 3: Unit Economics and Business Models Matter – A Lot

One thing we got right at Health at Hand was having a deep understanding of the economics of the healthcare system and telehealth.

Health at Hand wasn't just about connecting patients and doctors, it was about building a scalable business model where each consultation made sense financially.

CONCLUSION

We quickly learned that a great product is only as good as the economics driving it. In the current environment, entrepreneurs need to think beyond B2C revenue. The API economy and platform effects are redefining what a successful digital-health business looks like. By integrating with insurance companies, hospitals and even consumer wearables, ensure your own telehealth product becomes a critical node in a much larger healthcare ecosystem.

Embed your product into the system and you will find long term partners and sticky revenue.

So, what's next for the digital healthcare sector?

AI-POWERED HEALTHCARE: AI-driven diagnostics and virtual health assistants are making telehealth more efficient. The next digital healthcare unicorns will use AI not just to streamline consultations, but to predict patient needs, helping doctors intervene before a problem worsens. Remember, predictive and preventative healthcare not only saves costs, but also lives.

PERSONALISED MEDICINE & DATA: with wearable tech and genetic data, healthcare is becoming increasingly personalised. Digital health platforms that can process and act on massive datasets to offer customised treatment will win the market – particularly if they can focus on finding individually tailored patient solutions before people get sick. We will all experience our own unique healthcare problems that require their own bespoke solutions.

GLOBAL HEALTH ECOSYSTEM INTEGRATION: don't just think local; think global. Platforms that can integrate into different healthcare systems, comply with multiple regulatory environments and offer cross-border care, will thrive. As I learnt from my time in San Francisco, think big and think global.

The future belongs to those who can innovate not just from a technology perspective, but also with business models, legislation and patient experience.

Starting my own business was about so much more than just making money: I learnt an immeasurable amount about myself and others, I collected skills I still don't quite appreciate I have (I am certainly no engineer, but I possibly understand more than I give myself credit for) and I wear the scars of endless micro-failures – something we all need in life to make us better people and allow us to grow.

In times of self-reflection, I am upset that I never really gave myself the option to sell the business on my own terms – instead, it was a scrambled sale prompted by a lack of cashflow and an ever-depleting runway. Equally importantly, I wasn't able to quite have the impact on people's lives that I would have liked.

I often focus on the missed opportunities, and the feeling of not capitalising on a clear inflection point for the digital healthcare sector. It would be remiss of me not to mention that twelve months after I sold the business, the Covid pandemic emerged and transformed the whole telehealth sector from being a nice-to-have to a must-have. Timing, as they say, is everything.

Despite facing numerous challenges, I am incredibly proud to have successfully scaled a business that I founded to serve over four million patients across six countries in the emerging markets. Numerous telehealth businesses before and since have failed to return any money to their shareholders, and the sale of Health at Hand to a Fortune 500 company was a significant milestone, not least because we had built a robust enough business to pass Allianz's rigorous due-diligence process. This was a testament to the strong operational foundation we built, ensuring that we adhered to global standards in data privacy, storage and clinical protocols.

Looking back, I know we made the right decision in selling to Allianz over Babylon. Today, Health at Hand thrives as an in-house cost-containment tool for Allianz, enabling millions more patients to access high-quality medical care in an instant, and I take great pride in knowing that the Health at Hand brand continues to thrive today.

Additionally, I am deeply grateful to my colleagues and shareholders who stood by me throughout this journey. Our team's remarkably low staff turnover during my time, coupled with the successful careers many of my team members have gone on to build since, are accomplishments I hold in high regard. As a business, we plucked a number of talented individuals from a life of relative obscurity in inner-city Karachi and have since seen them take on executive engineering roles in some of the largest companies in the world, relocating to the likes of Singapore and San Francisco.

I am also still in touch with many of my shareholders, who were unwaveringly supportive throughout, some of whom are ready to commit capital to my next project, believing there is no better person to run a business than someone who has faced such challenges and come out the other side.

But what I am most proud of is that collectively, as a team, we made a real and positive difference to the lives of thousands of individuals and across an immeasurable number of communities in the markets in which we operated: labour-camp workers in Dubai, oil-rig workers in Abu Dhabi, rural communities in Saudi Arabia and the elderly in Oman. We really did improve their access to healthcare, and in a real sense we changed their lives for the better.

My Health at Hand journey was never about the money. It was about doing something that made a positive impact on people's lives, and in that sense it was a success. Millions more people were given access to primary healthcare through our work.

Will I do it again? Sure as hell I will. And with all I've learnt, I believe my next venture is likely to have an even greater impact.

Secretly, I'm still dreaming of unicorns!

> 'Risk more than others think is safe.
> Dream more than others think is practical'
>
> **HOWARD SCHULTZ,**
> **CEO OF STARBUCKS**

FURTHER READING

Below is a list of books mentioned in the text that I found particularly useful or inspirational while building Health at Hand:

Clark, Simon and Will Louch – *The Key Man* (2021)
Coll, Steve – *The Bin Ladens: An Arabian Family in the American Century* (2008)
Gladwell, Malcolm – *Outliers* (2009)
Hemingway, Ernest – *The Sun Also Rises* (1926)
Kahneman, Daniel – *Thinking, Fast and Slow* (2012)
Komisar, Randy – *Getting to Plan B* (2009), *I Fucking Love That Company* (2015), and *Straight Talk for Startups* (2018)
Peale, Norman Vincent – *The Power of Positive Thinking* (1952)
Sinek, Simon – *Leaders Eat Last: Why Some Teams Pull Together and Others Don't* (2017)
Taplin, Jonathan – *Move Fast and Break Things* (2018)
Topol, Eric – *The Patient Will See You Now* (2015)
Voss, Chris – *Never Split the Difference* (2016)

ACKNOWLEDGEMENTS

I've done my best to recall the events and conversations in this book as faithfully as possible. If there are any inaccuracies, they are unintentional and entirely my fault. While I accept responsibility for any missteps made during Health at Hand's journey, the credit for every success belongs to the remarkable team whose hard work, belief and collaboration made it all possible.

There are so many people I owe thanks to, and if I've accidentally missed anyone in the list that follows, it's entirely by mistake – every contribution, big or small, has meant everything to me.

Nadim, you deserve to be first on this list. You've been an absolute rockstar in my life ever since we met at university. One of the brightest, kindest and most brilliant people I know. Thank you for your friendship, your wisdom, your unwavering support – and for all the incredible times we've shared, with so many more still to come.

To Amy – thank you for believing in me and in Health at Hand from the very beginning. For being my late-night red-wine partner-in-crime and for the sacrifices you made along the way. Your friendship means the world.

To Jenna – though your Health at Hand journey ended too soon, it was a privilege to have you on the team, however briefly, and I have no doubt your star will keep rising.

Aftab, what would I have done without you? I learnt so much from you through every stage of the journey. Your steady hand kept me grounded, and I'm so proud of everything you've gone on to achieve since. Here's hoping our career paths cross again one day.

Sameer, thank you for your kindness, your friendship and your unshakable commitment to the mission. Health at Hand changed for the better the moment you walked through the door, and I'll always be grateful for everything you gave to the cause.

Thank you to Dr Yasmine for professionalising Health at Hand and ensuring that clinical quality was at the heart of everything we did.

A big thank you to Shiju for always being just a phone call or email away, for consistently delivering brilliant design work for Health at Hand and countless other projects, and for creating the chart that appears on page 172.

Thank you to Dr Becky and Dr Ruhil for your bravery in being the first two doctors we hired, and for the patience you showed in waiting for our user numbers to grow.

Thank you to Gaurav for your inspirational branding and marketing vision – your creativity gave Health at Hand a voice and a personality far beyond what I could have imagined.

To Christian – you'll always have a special place in this story as our first and largest client. Thank you for placing your trust in me and in Health at Hand; I am beyond grateful for your belief in what we were building.

And a huge thank you to Pat and your wonderful wife, Kelly – what a wedding that was, by the way! You inspired me from our first meeting, and it was your belief in me that gave me the confidence to take the leap and start Health at Hand. I'll always be deeply grateful for that.

ACKNOWLEDGEMENTS

Thank you to Fadi and the team at Blackbox for such an inspirational two weeks in San Francisco. And to my 'BBC 24' cohort.

Thank you to the Dubai Health Authority for being true to your vision of being a progressive and technology-first health authority and for being regional telehealth pioneers.

Thank you to expert presenter and friend Georgia Tolley for inviting me to the Dubai Eye studios for multiple radio interviews and for kindly providing a preview of your questions ahead of time.

Thank you to the late Richard Field, my English teacher, whose creative bribery tactics (involving beer) introduced me to the joy of reading and writing. No teacher ever inspired me more.

A big thank you to Charlie Inglefield for sharing your insights into life as an author, and for taking the time to thoughtfully critique my original book proposal – your guidance made a real difference.

Thanks to PJ, Jeremy, Marcus, Annabel, Guy and Marko for your amazing friendship. And to Tony and Sarah, thank you for the belief you had in me.

Thank you to Nick Cowley for kindly lending me Tim Roupell's brilliant book *Bread and Butter* – and, in doing so, unknowingly introducing me to the wonderful team at Quartet.

A huge thank you to my publicist, Grace Pilkington, for your guidance and for your work in championing a naive debut author's book and for teaching me how the publishing world works.

I'm immensely grateful to Ian Hyland for taking a chance on my unsolicited book proposal – I recall our first meeting in the *Spectator*'s mews office in Westminster with huge fondness.

And to John Walsh, Managing Editor at Quartet, thank you for believing in me and for giving this story a home.

It would be completely remiss of me not to acknowledge the huge role played by Peter Jacobs, my kind, patient and thoughtful editor. Thank you for trusting my voice, for providing the guiding hand I absolutely needed to complete this book, and for making the process of writing *Dreaming of Unicorns* an incredibly enjoyable one.

To my parents – thank you Mum and Dad for giving me such a wonderful education and for sacrificing so much to do so. Thank you for bringing me up in such a loving and supportive home and, most importantly, for giving me the wings and confidence to chase my dreams of living abroad and building my own business.

To Lucy, Rich, and your wonderful children – thank you for your constant counsel, your support and the love that's always been felt, no matter the distance.

To Claire, my truly incredible wife – your unwavering kindness, patience and love teach me something new every single day. I am endlessly grateful for your constant support and belief in me – and for all you do for our family.

And to my three wonderful children, Raff, Willa and Monty – you inspire me daily, fill my world with joy and give me every reason to push harder and be better. I could not be more proud of you all.

And finally to you, the reader – thank you for investing your time and hard-earned money in this book. I hope you've enjoyed the story and maybe found a lesson or two in my experiences. If it inspires the next wave of entrepreneurs to chase their ambitions, that will be my greatest reward.

Be curious, be brave, be kind.